A Comic Vision
of
Self-Government

Essays About Political Ideas Shaped
and Illuminated by Wisdom Literature

by Alan Griesinger

For Julie, Peter, and Michael,
with love

Copyright ©2016, Alan Griesinger

A Comic Vision of Self-Government: Essays About Political Ideas Shaped and Illuminated by Wisdom Literature

All Rights Reserved. No part of this publication may be reproduced, stored in a retrieval system or transmitted in any form by any means electronic, mechanical, or photocopying, recording or otherwise without the permission in writing from the publisher.

Requests for permission to make copies of any part of the work should be submitted online at info@mascotbooks.com or mailed to Mascot Books, 560 Herndon Parkway #120, Herndon, VA 20170.

Library of Congress Control Number: 2016910051
ISBN-13: 9781631778155
CPSIA Code: PBANG1116A

Printed in the United States

www.mascotbooks.com

A Comic Vision
of
Self-Government

Essays About Political Ideas Shaped
and Illuminated by Wisdom Literature

by Alan Griesinger

CONTENTS

PREFACE

On March 15th, 2015 I posted on my website "A Comic Vision in India," the first essay in this volume. It records impressions from our two weeks there in January. Near the end of the essay I address the terrible inefficiency and waste of public resources we witnessed which was crystallized for us on the road north to Agra. Along the route, mile after mile, truncated overpasses of a superhighway pointlessly littered the landscape, for they had no road to connect them. The project had been abandoned years ago. Life, however, had not abandoned the old road; it was full of traffic, people getting where they needed to go. They still streamed around the bridges to nowhere that the political class had built. That was a year ago, and since then a Presidential election has forced us as a country to confront the effect on popular sentiment of arrogance and costly mistakes in own politics. The passions stirred by the campaigns have brought home the question posed by our trip to India about that which enables a nation to survive and prosper despite the taxing missteps which mark the lives of human beings.

The rest of the essays in this volume, posted on my website in succession throughout the year, argue that the political ideas of Adam Smith, Edmund Burke, and Paul Johnson have compelling answers to that question, for these writers present a comic vision of self-government based on the natural attractions of relationship and the truth. The alternative, of course, is a vision which can only come into being through coercion and deception. To resolve the question closer to the way it was resolved when the country was founded, we need to reestablish in the culture the models of true self-government that made self-government a reality in the first place.

I confess that, since I was an English teacher, I have a bias in favor of my subject as a vehicle for this project, for literature discovers the root of self-government in the everyday interactions of Everyman. These essays, like the readings of "The Knight's Tale" and *A Midsummer Night's Dream* in my first book, would restore the life, the rich texture, and the bright colors of what I refer to as wisdom literature, for it still has the power to impress present and future generations with sound models. Through a process of natural selection, texts like Genesis, Job, and Proverbs in the Old Testament, *The Odyssey* of Homer, the Epistles of Paul in the New Testament, and the works of Chaucer and Shakespeare have survived from generation to generation as guides for getting the most out of life. And with good reason. They and the political ideas they have shaped are the standard around which free people gather.

In the old days poets like Homer began their work by expressing their gratitude to the muses for inspiration and guidance without which their poem would not exist. In the same spirit I express my gratitude for the good books by Russ Roberts, Matt Ridley, Thomas Sowell, Yuval Levin, and Paul Johnson that I review in the essays. They have inspired and guided an inquiry into the question.

April 2016

Jacob left Beersheba and set out for Harran.

When he reached a certain place, he stopped for the night because the sun had set.
Taking one of the stones there, he put it under his head and
lay down to sleep.

He had a dream in which he saw a stairway resting on the earth,
with its top reaching to heaven, and the angels of God
were ascending and descending on it.

~ Genesis 28: 10-12

Does not wisdom call out?
Does not understanding raise her voice?

At the highest point along the way,
where the paths meet, she takes her stand;

beside the gate leading into the city,
at the entrance, she cries aloud:

"To you, O people, I call out;
I raise my voice to all mankind."

~ Proverbs 8:1-4

Who hopes for what they already have?
But if we hope for what we do not have, we wait for it patiently.

~ Romans 8: 24-25

Anyone but a fool knows, in his soul,
That every part derives from this great whole.
For nature cannot be supposed to start
From some particular portion or mere part.

~ Chaucer, "The Knight's Tale"

This thou perceiv'st, which makes thy love more strong
To love that well, which thou must leave ere long.

~ Shakespeare, Sonnet 73

Chapter One:

A Comic Vision in India

Warwick Goble's
Sita Finds Rama Among the Lotus Blooms

In January of 2015 my wife and I traveled to India for the first time. It's one thing to stand before the spellbinding beauty of the Taj. We have done that with other buildings in other places. It's something else altogether to see thousands of people, mile after mile after mile, living along the roadsides in India. The experience turns our Western ideas of poverty to dust and ashes. Along with the shock of it, though, was a sense that, quite apart from how we might feel about what we were seeing, we were witnessing a functioning, albeit a very different, society.

Unlike our Western passion for privacy, the people lining the roadsides live in the open—brushing their teeth, eating on the ground, working, defecating, warming their hands by a small fire, carrying water, carrying a baby. They are busy doing their own thing, and yet the densely populated scene as a whole conveys a sense of purpose. Also, it includes openings to the future. At night, there are wedding processions in the crowded streets attended by hundreds and brilliantly lit with flood lights. In working class neighborhoods we see children walking to school in attractive uniforms.

Along the sacred river Ganges there's the same nakedness of individuals acting on their own while acting out timeless rituals. Even in winter they remove their outer garments on the steps of the ghat—leaving their things with a priest for safekeeping—and then descend to be immersed, to have the water on their skin (and feel the blood rush to the surface, as one woman explained). It's a long day's work for Ganga-gi. Every day at dusk the priests begin the rite that puts the river to sleep. As darkness falls, they chant ancient verses, blow the conches, light the incense, and brandish the torches—all in traditional gestures. The life of the fire, the rawness of it in the dark, reminds us that life is an unbroken chain of sacrifices: the oil in the torch giving itself up to fuel the fire, plants and animals giving up their life to feed others, our ancestors sacrificing themselves to give us a secure life in a secure nation, just as we sacrifice our time and labor to sustain the lives of children. And then a short walk from where the river is put to sleep, on the ghat where the cremations take place day and night, the lightly covered bodies of the dead are completely exposed to a fire that rushes to transform them into heat, smoke, and ash. It takes a few hours; the priest, the body's relatives, and all of us watching from the river are there to sanctify and to witness this final life's lesson.

We were warned that driving in India is "controlled chaos." It's certainly chaotic at all times, but the "controlled" part is only true if you make it safely to your destination. We shared the road, even major highways, with pedestrians, cyclists, motorcycles with four people somehow sandwiched on the seat, rickshaws, lorries large and small, tractors pulling wagonloads of produce and people, and of course the sacred cows who own the road. These things go at their own pace, but for those of us in cars they were all opponents in high speed games of chicken (even with cows!) no matter which way they were going. There may be rules of the road, but our astute Indian driver was the only one in our car who knew what they were. His artful dodging kept us riveted for a long and harrowing afternoon on the roads north to Agra. After being so exposed and vulnerable, our party ate and drank heartily that night. For me, our afternoon and evening on the road touched on the questions posed by what I'd seen in Delhi and Varanassi: "What holds this place together? Why is it still working?" Whether we liked it or not and with our life on the line, for an afternoon in our little car we had become part of the warp and woof of things in India, weaving in out of an endless stream of traffic.

Years ago I had studied books on India and Hinduism. Before we left home, I rummaged through my shelves and took two books with me on the trip to read when I had the chance, R.K. Narayan's translation of *The Ramayana* and Juan Mascaro's translation of *The Bhagavad Gita*. At our first hotel in Delhi we had a little free time in the afternoon so I went to the lounge and ordered coffee at the bar. I had brought *The Ramayana* with me and was reading it while I waited. The young man behind the bar inquired about the book, and when I showed it to him, his demeanor completely changed, as if a light had been turned on inside. He was delighted that I was acquainted with the story, and he told stories about the role it played in his and his community's life. A day later I went to the lounge once again to have coffee and relax. This time I sat in a different place and was served by young woman. She greeted me as "the one reading the Ramayana" even though I didn't remember seeing her the day before.

Sometimes we rode from city to city in a large bus. We felt safer there, a match for size with the thousands of lorries we encountered both coming and going. Lorries in India are more like massive movie stars than trucks. Their surfaces have a texture like woven fabric and are painted like a brightly colored sari; the mirrors and fenders are decorated with talismantic tassels; and at night lorries are lit up like Christmas trees. Because our vantage point was as high as their cabs, I could look into them as we passed them or they passed us. Inside the cab riding along with the driver there were those brightly colored pictures of male and female gods and goddesses. Working men on the roads of India wear their religion on their sleeves, as it were. Now that I've been on those roads, I can see why. The Greek philosopher Thales wrote that "All things are full of gods." These cabs and our experience of India as a whole manifested the idea in such a colorful and concrete way. What else can one conclude when you look at the surface of a temple that's completely covered with carved images of immortals.

For several months I read and considered the questions our trip to India had raised. I discovered in the Sanskrit literature of the Vedas, the Upanishads, Sankhya, Vedanta, and Tantra a basic correspondence with the comic vision that's the subject of my work on Chaucer and Shakespeare. For example, in his book on Hinduism Stephen Cross quotes the story from the Rig Veda about two birds on one tree. He uses it to describe the two realms that are consistently delineated in Sanskrit literature: that "of empirical existence and ordinary knowing, the world of name and form; and behind it, that quite different order to which the mind doesn't have access and which is Brahman—or, when spoken of in relation to man, Atman":

Two Birds with fair wings, knit with bonds of friendship

In the same sheltering tree have found a refuge.

One of the twain eats the sweet Figtree's fruitage;

The other, eating not, regardeth only.

Near the end of his book, he sums up his very readable survey with this conclusion: "Informing the whole of Hinduism is the idea of release or moksha. It is essentially a change of identity," from being the bird that eats the figtree's fruitage to the one that watches.

The relationship between these two realms is also the subject of *A Comic Vision of Great Constancy.* In *A Midsummer Night's Dream* Helena touches on this theme when she complains that she suffers in relationship with Demetrius because "Love looks, not with the eyes, but with the mind." People look with the mind to determine what a thing is. There's a strong desire to know the object, but this looking is conditioned by the cultural and personal bias of the knower. Looking with the eyes, on the other hand, wonders at the fact that the object exists at all. In this looking, life is a miracle—"to be" illuminated by "not to be." So it's a strange and even irrational way of looking, like seeing that the world is full of gods, and yet teachers and writers for thousands of years have willed us their assurance that it can be done. In comedy, it's as simple as slipping on a banana peel because we are busy texting, a variation on an old burlesque routine. In these experiences the thing which absorbed our attention is swallowed up by the whole from which it derives, the "thing" we had been ignoring. Like waking from a dream, we land willy nilly on a larger intelligence, a starting point for fresh eyes. This is clearly not the omniscience of a god, but it's something: it's the beginning of wisdom for a lifetime of being a beginner.

A Comic Vision of Great Constancy and these essays argue that the wisdom literature of the world still has a vital role to play in the government of our lives. This is particularly true in a society run by technocrats and experts, for wisdom depends on acknowledging the greatness of what we don't know. In India we saw terrible waste—building after building half finished and abandoned, a whole series of overpasses constructed years ago but with no road to connect them, a crazy patchwork tax system that ties up traffic at borders between states, the mounting evidence of poor planning, terrible gaps in political continuity, and, we were told, rampant corruption. So what to do? The people of India have been figuring this out for centuries. Life still streams around the bridges to nowhere that the administrative state has built.

But we didn't find the cynicism, the dark humor that's a staple in other badly run countries we have visited, like Russia, for example. Instead, there's a brightness and vitality that's quite the opposite. Having turned for my own health and happiness as a teacher, parent, and husband to the wisdom literature of the West and East, I'm inclined to attribute the lively pulse of India to a love of ancient stories, their main characters (like the loyal and resourceful monkey god, Hanuman), and the life lessons these stories embody. Juan Mascaro informs the reader quite early in his Introduction that there is no tragedy in Sanskrit literature. On the whole, he writes, it's "a romantic literature interwoven with idealism and practical wisdom, and with a passionate longing for spiritual vision." This describes the literature I have written about and which I call a comic vision. No wonder, then, there were so many books I wanted to read in the bookstore at the Delhi airport, my last stop before boarding the plane.

Chapter Two:
The Comic Vision of Adam Smith

Nicolas Poussin's *Echo and Narcissus*

How to Get the Most out of Life

In *How Adam Smith Can Change Your Life*, Russ Roberts argues that Smith's first book, *The Theory of Moral Sentiments*, has timeless insights into human nature and civil society that will amply repay the time and effort one invests in studying them. Roberts has "translated" the much longer original into a modern idiom with many modern illustrations, but he bases his commentary on selected passages of Smith's actual prose so the reader can hear the master himself in his own voice.

In the introduction Roberts notes that, forty years after Smith published his book, he revised it shortly before he died even though he wasn't doing much serious scholarship. Roberts then ventures a guess as to why Smith returned to its themes: "Once you start to think about human motivation and the bright and dark side of humanity—what Faulkner called the 'human heart in conflict with itself'—it's hard to think of anything else. Trying to understand your neighbor and, in turn, yourself, really doesn't get old." In addition to underscoring Smith's and Roberts's own motivation, the observation explains why a student of wisdom literature might begin essays on self-government with his book on Adam Smith, why readers continue to study books like this, and why I invested so heavily in the two authors I write about in *A Comic Vision of Great Constancy*.

The quote is a passionate assertion about that which moves Smith, Faulkner, and Roberts himself to study and write. Roberts, who is an economist, has been persuaded by *The Theory of Moral Sentiments* that economics is not just about money and merchandise. It's about the getting the most out of life. To do that we have to understand ourselves and those around us, and this requires a thorough acquaintance with our passions, our "sentiments." These are subjects we associate more with literature so it's no wonder that I might find myself intrigued and at home with Adam Smith's book about what makes people tick.

The quote from Faulkner puts in mind a person who is "wrestling" with a difficult question. This image prepares the reader for one of Roberts' and Smith's most important points about how to get the most out of life. Ancient literature depicts the wrestling or the fighting of man against man where one forces the other to take a fall. The *Iliad* is filled with these contests, and they are the combatants' vehicle for achieving the material rewards of victory and the spiritual reward of undying fame. The comic vision of wisdom literature, however, transforms the nature of the contest. Instead of fighting a man or a monster, a comic hero like Odysseus has to wrestle with the promptings of his own fierce pride and the consequences of when it asserts itself.

For example, the pride of Odysseus suffers a terrible defeat when he and his crew are trapped in the cave of the man-eating Cyclops, Polyphemus. When asked his name, Odysseus tells the monster that he is Nobody. It's a private joke (in a desperate situation), and Odysseus may think that it will save his actual name from the shame of defeat. Later, after he manages to escape, his pride gets the better of him. He boasts to Polyphemus that it was Odysseus who blinded him and escaped, but, once given this intelligence, Polyphemus can call on his father Zeus to curse that name. The rest of the story tells how Odysseus expiates the curse, the dark stain on his name. The trials come to a climax when the lightning bolt of Zeus destroys his ship, and he loses all the outward trappings of his kingship as a naked man adrift on a vast ocean. Many adventures later on his own island of Ithaca, he wears the trappings of a beggarly Nobody—a character who, like light, is virtually invisible, who illuminates like light in a cave the reality of the situation, and who can act with intelligence and great courage to mend it.

Odysseus won renown among the Greeks as a mighty wrestler. He won the respect of the gods and a pathway home as a man who is compelled to wrestle with himself.

A Summary of How Adam Smith
Can Change Your Life

A. The Impartial Spectator and the Veil of Self-Delusion

For centuries storytellers from East and West have described the many ways characters wrestle with choices, and in *The Theory of Moral Sentiments* Adam Smith has written his variation on the human heart in conflict with itself. What follows in this summary of Roberts' book freely borrows words, phrases, and quotes from him. Human beings, argues Smith, are inalienably self-interested. At the same time, it's also true that human beings don't always act out of self interest. What makes this difference? Our behavior in the end, argues Smith, is driven by an imaginary interaction with an impartial spectator; he alone can humble and teach us. Borrowing imagery from *The Odyssey* (this is my device, not that of Mr. Roberts), I venture that the impartial spectator is like the beggar Nobody who, owning nothing, has nothing to lose and who consists of nothing to which a bias can attach. The two characters, Polyphemus and Nobody, together represent the conflict Smith describes. The one-eyed Cyclops lacks perspective; he can only be self-interested. The impartial spectator, represented imaginatively by Homer as Nobody, sees the whole, not parts (or partials). To sum up, we are all self-interested human beings, but we are capable of acting honorably and nobly to satisfy what we imagine is the standard set by an impartial spectator. This describes the mechanics of the conflict, but, crucially, it doesn't tell us the origin and the enforcement of an honorable, noble standard. That comes next in Roberts' presentation of Smith's theory.

According to Smith, we learn the standard from our interactions with other people, for along with being inalienably self-interested we are inalienably social. This leads to an important assumption which is the foundation of Smith's moral theory. He writes, "Man naturally desires, not only to be loved, but to be lovely." He means "loved" in the fullest sense, and by "lovely" he means that the person loved merits being loved. There's no gap between the appearance and the reality of the person loved. If the statement is true, then we depend on others for our good opinion of ourselves. Because it's a great happiness to be loved and a great misery to be hated (and to know that we deserve the one or the other), we are held in check by those who judge us, and in time we do this imaginatively for ourselves through the device of an impartial spectator who overlooks our actions.

In this vision, the operation of morality is a constant, active process deeply embedded in everyday interactions. Unfortunately, Smith's natural moral "system" often enough fails to work. For example, it gets short circuited when the feedback is merely the flattery of a self-interested party. More significantly, it breaks down altogether when a person's impartial spectator is no longer impartial. Like Odysseus defending his pride with a false name (How many ferociously ambitious politicians represent themselves to the public and to themselves as humble nobodies!), the impartial spectator surrenders to a fierce desire to be loved and issues a false report. To justify a selfish act, Smith explains, the corrupted spectator will cover the selfishness of the act with a "veil of self-delusion." Unfortunately, fooling ourselves in this way is just as easy and maybe even easier than fooling others. The strong desire to think that we are lovely in the eyes of others keeps us from repairing our behaviors.

B. The Remedy: Observing Imperfections in the Conduct of Others

So what's the "remedy"? Roberts supplies a quote from Smith which at first only hints at the way forward:

> *This self deceit, this fatal weakness of mankind, is the source of half the disorders of human life. If we saw ourselves in the light in which others see us, or in which they would see us if they know all, a reformation would generally be unavoidable. We could not otherwise endure the sight.*

These are big "if's." We easily fool ourselves, and our neighbors are easily fooled. Because of this the system breaks down. But Smith then points to a cure:

> Nature, however, has not left this weakness, which is of so much importance, altogether without a remedy; nor has she abandoned us entirely to the delusions of self-love. Our continual observations upon the conduct of others, insensibly lead us to form to ourselves certain general rules concerning what is fit and proper either to be done or to be avoided.

In a surprising (and comic) reversal of fortunes, our neighbors' imperfections help us to see our own. These norms, Smith believes, over time help the impartial spectator to master the impulses of self-love.

Smith recognizes that rooting out self-deception can be difficult and painful, but he is encouraging us to take that step:

> He is a bold surgeon, they say, whose hand does not tremble when he performs an operation upon his own person; and he is equally bold who does not hesitate to pull off the mysterious veil of self-delusion, which covers from his view the deformities of his own conduct.

It's what a good man, a healer, does to recover his health. Smith has visually dramatized the moment. The mind forged manacles of self-delusion can only be unfastened by the mind that forged and put them on in the first place. Smith would praise the healer's courage, and so he plays the role of a friend encouraging a neighbor who wrestles with self-delusion. Neighbors can play this positive role as well as the flattering one.

C. Fleshing Out the Theory with Conventional Wisdom

The chapter on self-delusion comes in the middle of the book. Acknowledging confirmation bias, a modern term for self-delusion, is a critical step in getting the most out of life, but Roberts has much to add that fleshes out Smith's theory. These chapters contain advice about living in the world that's similar to the worldly wisdom of Proverbs. For example,

Smith warns against the seductions of wealth, fame, and power. It's a mistake to think that these things make us lovely. Instead, he advises, pursue wisdom and goodness. To begin with, a person must act appropriately, for propriety gains the approval of those around you. Smith defines it, not as fashion or etiquette, but as matching our emotional responses to the emotions of others. When you share emotions at the right level of intensity, he argues, it builds trust, and this is the beginning of loveliness.

Propriety gains the approval of others, but people chiefly admire and celebrate virtue, which Smith divides into three parts. Prudence involves taking care of yourself, your health and well-being; justice involves not harming others; and beneficence involves being good to others. All this is perfectly well known; it's a form of conventional wisdom. These are rules or norms that human beings have learned for centuries through interactions with family, friends, and neighbors. They are as true now as they were thousands of years ago. Our family, friends, and neighbors are still teaching them to us; they are a natural part of human experience.

D. An Unplanned Orderliness and Logic

After presenting Smith's advice about following the path of wisdom and virtue, Roberts ventures to describe what he judges to be Smith's most important contribution to the study of human nature and social phenomena. He begins this section with ten pages of examples—like the public's adoption of the word "google" in popular usage and fashion trends that dictate the wearing of hats and the clothes we wear—which he employs to make the argument that "many aspects of our lives look orderly but are under no one's control." Everyone's decisions together "decide" whether "google" will be used in popular speech and whether men, as a general rule, wear hats.

Roberts has collected his own examples to illustrate what lies behind Smith's theory, which came so naturally to him that he didn't discuss the phenomena in a general sense. Smith would persuade us that we are all part of a natural moral order like that which determines what words we use and what clothes we wear. It's for this reason that we can make the world a better place without resorting to the mechanics of legislatures, laws, and official police forces. Whether it's stated explicitly or not, Roberts and Smith argue that a coherent, moral order can emerge out of countless individual decisions and actions, where social phenomena have "an orderliness and logic to them even though they are not designed consciously by an individual." Our individual actions, though infinitesimally small in the overall scheme of things, do make a difference in the aggregate. We can make the world a better place by being wise and virtuous, for we all have a hand in the invisible hand that creates a civil society.

The first part of Roberts' book develops the implications around Smith's assumption that "Man naturally desires, not only to be loved, but to be lovely." The final three chapters develop the implications around this last assumption that the acts of individuals can make the world a better place without everyone following a government script. Adam Smith, Roberts tells us, "occasionally has good things to say about government intervention," but he strongly opposed what now would be called "industrial policy." He especially disliked the man of system, described by Roberts as "the leader with a scheme to remake society according to some master plan or vision." There are other ways, Smith believed, of changing the world than using legislation. The world is a far more complex place than is ever accounted for in their system, and Utopians can be very dangerous both before and after their schemes fail to work. According to Roberts, "Smith is reminding us that politics is not where life happens." *The Theory of Moral Sentiments*, Roberts concludes, describes how to get the most out of a life lived with family, friends, and neighbors—people in our immediate circle. His other book, *A Wealth of Nations*, is about living with people we don't know, and that's another story.

The Comic Visions of Smith and Shakespeare

A. The Boldness Required to Pull Off the Veil

At the beginning of the book Roberts gives a charming account of reading *The Theory of Moral Sentiments* for the first time. He was more or less forced into it, but once fully engaged, Adam Smith's vision completely won him over. Smith's ideas make him consider more carefully everyday decisions concerning work and family. In the fifth chapter Roberts imagines visiting the great man himself on a rainy night in Edinburgh, and he ends the book by describing the end of that imaginary visit. I recognize the device, for I do much the same thing at the end of *A Comic Vision of Great Constancy*. I imagine Shakespeare looking at me, and his eyes are like "windows opening on an invitation: make friends with me, and you may make friends with the world and yourself." Writers like Chaucer and Shakespeare speak with the authority of a seasoned counselor. Their words begin to have, if not a human shape, then the strong impression of a human heart and mind.

I find much in Smith that corresponds with the comic vision of Homer, Chaucer, and Shakespeare. Comic characters are invariably self-interested, and yet the form of comedy brings these characters to a point where they can be tractable members of a civil society. Traditional comedies end in a marriage, and marriage, perhaps more than any other institution, has schooled both men and women for thousands of years in the limits of self-interest. It's significant that *A Midsummer Night's Dream* ends with the consummation of three marriages. Adam Smith's "system" relies on an impartial spectator to guide us into the graces of a civil society, but, as Smith himself admits, this figure is not always impartial. Like the human being whose behaviors it monitors, it sometimes falls into an enchanted but frozen limbo of love-for-an-image, loses its impartiality, and fails to steer the person it governs away from self love. The catatonia of love has long been noted in Western literature. Ancient Greeks depicted the state with great exactness in the story of Narcissus forever gazing at his own image in a pool of water, and the immobilization caused by this kind of love informs the stories of Chaucer and Shakespeare.

Shakespeare framed *A Midsummer Night's Dream* around the theme of self-love by putting the innocent egotist Bottom at the center of the narrative. Bottom is the eternal diva at the bottom of Everyman who plays the self-appointed star of the universe. He would hog the spotlight and play all the parts. Robin's alchemy teaches Bottom that he's an ass for thinking and acting this way, and, while Bottom never fully acknowledges his true state as an ass, the hint of it is enough to transform him into a gentleman. Bottom's story gives us hope. Falstaff's impartial spectator, on the other hand, must have died an early death, for Falstaff himself shamelessly revels in false reports. Nevertheless, he was Shakespeare's most beloved character in his own time, and audiences still love him because his lies and self-justifications are as palpably gross and obvious as his physical bulk. They make him immensely human.

Self-deception is so much easier than self-knowledge. Earlier I quoted Smith's assertion that true self-knowledge is like performing surgery on oneself. It takes boldness, he writes, "to pull off the mysterious veil of self-delusion." True enough, but it takes so much boldness that hardly anyone does it on his own, especially in the early going as one confronts the overwhelming power of an attachment to one's own image. Smith's surgeon is very rare. In the stories of Homer, Chaucer, and Shakespeare life itself has to strip the veil, much like the two swindlers relieve the emperor of his clothes in Anderson's remarkable fable. Life then has the little boy cry out, "But the emperor has no clothes!" It will indeed require some courage for the emperor to admit that he stands before his people completely naked, but life has created the necessary conditions for him to confront it. The emperor entrenched in self-deception must make the final decision to surrender to the truth, but a Narcissistic self-love will exhaust all the other options first. This is what happens to the four lovers from Athens in *A Midsummer Night's Dream*. The fairy king Oberon and his chief minister

Robin arrange it so that, over the course of a helter-skelter night, the complete exhaustion of their bodies and minds (from the exercise of self-love) prepares them for the dreamless sleep that clarifies and renews their affections.

B. A Fatal Weakness and a Hateful Imperfection

Despite this difference, both Shakespeare and Smith have a keen appreciation for the danger that self-deception represents. Smith describes the veil of self-deceit as "a fatal weakness," and *A Midsummer Night's Dream* is constructed around an image quite similar to this veil. Just as Cupid wields a bow and an arrow to strike down his victims in the cause of Venus, Oberon places the juice of a little flower on the eyes of his victims so that they will madly dote on the next thing they see. Both the veil of self-deceit and the obsessive attachment to an object, however, are instances where love is dangerously misdirected as in the story of Narcissus. His obsessive attachment to his own image (and a narcissist like Bottom sees himself everywhere so he would be the next thing he sees) is a fatal short-circuiting of vision. The whole of life is left out, and so the pool has him in the end.

Just as Smith imagines an impartial spectator to counter the effects of self love on our vision, Oberon knows of another flower:

> *Whose liquor hath this virtuous property,*
> *To take from thence all error with his might*
> *And make his eyeballs roll with wonted sight.*

If only such a liquor existed! Nevertheless, just as we can imagine an impartial spectator, omniscience, and the whole from which all parts of the world derive, we can imagine and experience for ourselves a state where eyeballs roll with wonted sight. Throughout *A Comic Vision of Great Constancy* I make the case that human beings experience something like this in the wake-up call of a comic fall—that moment of wonder and surprise when people realize that an idea, to which they are violently attached, is just an idea and not reality. These moments open our eyes to things-as-they-are.

Oberon uses the liquor of this second flower to restore order in his kingdom, for the land in and around Athens has been overwhelmed by a flood of passions, including his own, that threatens everyone's health and safety. When he puts the anti-dote (that which neutralizes doting) on the eyes of his queen Titania, he calls the effects of the first liquor—the one that causes a person to obsessively dote on the next thing it sees (which for a narcissist will always be his own image)—"this hateful imperfection." I'm unable to say whether self-love is more accurately described as a fatal weakness or a hateful imperfection, but they are similar enough for me to believe that Shakespeare's inventions may have played a part in shaping Smith's theory of moral sentiments.

C. The Essence of a Comic Vision

Reading Roberts' account of their meeting, I'm inclined to picture Smith as Roberts depicts him, rather comfortably housed on a rainy night in a drafty but cozy room where there's a fire in the hearth, a strong draught of good Scotch for the visitor, and tea for the host. I'm inclined to picture Shakespeare, on the other hand, alone on a barren heath, blinded by driving rain, embittered and betrayed by those closest to him, and dimly aware that he has brought these things on himself. Shakespeare's tales suggest that human beings require something like a massive body blow or crack-up to wake us from the dream of self-deceit. Smith's account suggests that it's a rational process, the education a gentleman receives if he's serious about being a decent person, the sort of man Ben Franklin willed himself to be with his earnest programs of self-improvement.

I have recently read Brooke Allen's book about the founders of our country called *Moral Minority: Our Skeptical Founding Fathers.* The contrast that she presents in her book between Thomas Jefferson and John Adams reminds me of the contrast I find here between Smith and Shakespeare. Jefferson had an abiding faith in reason; it's his defining characteristic. Adams was every bit as intellectual as Jefferson, but he argued in a letter to Jefferson that philosophy will never govern vanity, pride, and revenge in human affairs. The apparent conflict between the two is resolved, however, when the concept of reason is opened up to include reason's fallibility, those missteps of mind that distort reality. We know from our own experience that human beings can still wake from dreams, reasonable or otherwise, that distort perception, and this, I believe, is the essence of the comic vision embodied in the works of Homer, Chaucer and Shakespeare.

It's a comic vision because we can draw meaning and direction for our lives from a study of them just as Adam Smith could in his time, and the study of these authors helps us to survive and prosper in our relationships. It's the promise and the hope of a vital and viable culture.

Chapter Three:
The Miracles of Comedy

Hendrick Martensz Sorgh's *The Vegetable Market*

The Flywheel That Drives Human Prosperity

The Rational Optimist: How Prosperity Evolves by Matt Ridley complements Russ Roberts' book in that they both derive from the work of Adam Smith. As a guide for our perplexing times Ridley's book is also like *A Conflict of Visions* by Thomas Sowell. First published in 1987, it still accurately describes *The Ideological Origins of Political Struggles*, its subtitle. Sowell's book is descriptive. He doesn't favor one side over the other in those political struggles. Instead, he aims at clarity. If you read it, you'll understand better why there is a conflict and why it's so intractable. Ridley also addresses a subject with great importance for modern politics. With the help of modern science, he narrates (in less than 400 pages) an epic that illuminates 200,000 years of human development. Ridley's book, however, is prescriptive. He explains "the flywheel" that has driven the rise in our human standard of living over that period, and his analysis favors exchange as a proven path for our survival and prosperity.

Ridley's argument is quite simple. Human beings, he writes, have prospered from prehistory into the present because they discovered through exchange the division of labor and the specialization that encourage innovation. "The more people can specialize and exchange," he writes, "the wealthier we will all be." He then supports his thesis with an impressive array of examples from all over the globe and from every era of human development. Ridley's version of this story gives us good, scientific reasons for why life is no longer as brutish and short as it used to be and for his optimism about the future.

He concludes the book with a chapter called "The Catallaxy," which is Frederich Hayek's word for "the spontaneous order created by exchange and specialization." Because Ridley quotes several times from Adam Smith's two books in his text, it's clear that he is an important influence. The catallaxy, the marketplace which Ridley defines and describes, is what informed me about him, for Russ Roberts' book has an endorsement by Matt Ridley on the dustcover. This little story demonstrates that a marketplace (of ideas, in this instance) comes into existence as a meeting place for people who want to get the most out of life. From an economic perspective, getting the most out of life means devising a system of exchange that allows the most efficient use of scarce resources, and experience has proven that a marketplace answers that need. But getting the most out of life doesn't just involve material things. Adam Smith continues to have such a powerful influence because the economic system he outlines in *The Wealth of Nations* is thoroughly grounded in *The Theory of Moral Sentiments*. We get more out of life, as the previous essay outlines, when we understand and acknowledge the moral order he describes there that underlies civil society.

Smith and Ridley are optimists because they have concluded from their research that exchange establishes a realistic basis for peace and prosperity which doesn't rely on coercion. Freedom, they believe, is a sounder basis for a social order. Unlike a law or an insistence on brotherly love, the act of exchanging doesn't force people to be kind; it teaches them to recognize that their self-interest lies in seeking cooperation. Summing up the significance of Smith's theories as an explanation for the civil peace associated with trade, Ridley writes that, "Smith brilliantly confused the distinction between altruism and selfishness: if sympathy allows you to please yourself by pleasing others, are you being selfish or altruistic?" Trade embeds altruistic effects in self-interested efforts.

Since he has access to the findings of twenty first century anthropology, Ridley supports Smith's basic insights with examples from human prehistory. There's sufficient archeological evidence to conclude that when potentially hostile tribes traded necessary goods, the custom gradually established relationships based on an exchange that benefits both sides rather than kinship or tribal loyalties. In this way the division of labor was extended not just to family members or strangers but to enemies. The process then developed for hundreds of thousands of years to the point where Smith could see that a citizen living in the 18th Century needed the assistance and cooperation of great multitudes.

To correct the notion that individuals and nations are more secure and happier when they are completely self-sufficient, Ridley has written a book that's a "Declaration of Interdependence." Like that other Declaration, he believes it to be a matter of great moment; hence there's urgency in his optimism. People need to know and fully appreciate that societies evolve prosperously only when they exchange freely with other populations. The economics of specialization explain why this is so. If one tribe can make fish hooks more efficiently than the tribe that's a more efficient producer of stone axes, they both profit in trade with each other. It's a non-zero sum bargain. Tribes that don't trade have to make everything themselves, and this is less efficient. Ridley supplies examples where people, like those on the island of Tasmania after it was separated from the mainland of Australia, over time lost the hunting and gathering skills they once employed to feed, shelter, and clothe themselves. In isolation these skills withered away, and the people were reduced to living virtually as naked men and women on the shore of a vast ocean.

Autonomy and a Web of Interdependence

I have written about this autonomy (symbolized by human nakedness) in *A Comic Vision of Great Constancy* and in the previous essays of this volume. Since I was an English teacher, I draw on examples from the humanities rather than the sciences for guidance concerning our personal and collective vulnerabilities. In the essay on Adam Smith I recall the nakedness of the Emperor when the child innocently points out to everyone that he has no clothes. Here's a man who is on his own in a very public way, and we are left to imagine the work he'll have of overcoming his self-deceptions once his subjects have seen such a graphic instance of it. Expelled from Eden, Adam and Eve (after God's initial help in covering their nakedness) labored in the world to provide food and shelter. In addition to the many theological and philosophical implications of the story, it suggests what everyone knows: that a boy and girl must leave the security of the nest and work in the world to become men and women. Similarly, in the life of our nation at a critical point the founders rebelled and declared their independence from the English crown, a move which exposed them to the military might of the empire. The declaration succeeded, but the United States has always been a work in progress within a global context.

The autonomy of an individual doesn't isolate him from the opinions of mankind or separate him from participation in world affairs. We learn this from the epic adventures of Odysseus. I've related that in one of those trials the sacker of cities is reduced to a naked man in a vast ocean for three days, but the narrative doesn't leave him in that state. He's destined to land on shore to reclaim his place as king of Ithaca and to reclaim Ithaca as a part of the larger world into which he has now been initiated. Nevertheless, even when he returns to his own island, Odysseus has learned from his experience that he will always be like a naked man in a vast ocean completely at the mercy of powers greater than his own. It's a bitter draught, but having drunk it he will rule more wisely than if he relied only on his own very limited powers. He now knows in the muscles and in the scorching fatigue of a body that has been buffeted by a vast ocean of experience that the world is a web of interdependence. Traversing unfamiliar terrains and seaways, he often had to rely on strangers (or the gods) who had better knowledge of the place to guide him on his way. On Ithaca, he depended on a few faithful friends to win the battle against the suitors.

The intelligence that informs the rule of Odysseus once he returns is the intelligence that lies behind Smith's *Theory of Moral Sentiments* and *The Wealth of Nations*. It's the light and warmth that radiates from what Hayek calls the catallaxy, but it's also what the Hebrew Bible calls a fear of the Lord. It's the Logos of Heraclitus, Philo, the Stoics, early Christians, and it's the wisdom that constitutes the comic vision of Chaucer, Shakespeare, and our own Constitution. All these forms of it admit the obvious. We are all autonomous human beings, and we are all equally limited in what we can know as an autonomous human being. Anyone who would get the most out of life has to take that into account. Even if we had a thousand eyes like Argus and an army of spies, we still wouldn't know every thing, and we might not know the one thing we need to know in order to survive and prosper. This doesn't mean, however, that the logos has gone missing. The voice of wisdom constantly calls out and reminds us that she is still there at the vital crossroad of our affairs even if an entire nation has lost sight of her. She can play a role in human affairs as long as there's one like Odysseus who has glimpsed her (as in his many encounters with Athene) for himself. When he tells his story to the Phaeacians, he reports how experiences in the world forced him to learn the greatness of what he didn't know, to survey as best he could the lay of the land, and to act prudently.

Like *The Odyssey* and the work of Adam Smith Ridley's book teaches how to get the most out of life. A good doctor who is familiar with the way the body works is more able to cure disease or to keep the body in good health. Like a good doctor, Ridley observes and prescribes. He knows from careful study and reliable evidence that exchange maintains and increases the health and prosperity of the body politic. Those that hinder exchange, like the pharaohs and high priests who sap the natural flow of exchange out of self-interest, are parasites that threaten the health of the body. It would be a mistake, however, to underestimate the natural powers of it. During World War II when the world was afflicted with totalitarian governments and total war, Ridley points to evidence that people continued to invent and create. Though gravely wounded, the catallaxy survived. This is why Ridley is an optimist.

A Wonderland of Human Ingenuity

Sometimes a book can have a magnetic effect on someone who comes into contact with it. Instead of a plain envelope with a plain message inside, the book is like the mirror that Alice passes through to encounter a wonderland. Usually, this is a trick that's easier for fiction, poetry, and drama to pull off, for these engage the imagination more directly. Even weeks after reading it, though, Ridley's nonfiction had that effect. When I go out shopping, humdrum encounters have a different quality. I'm grateful that all the drivers obey a few simple rules of the road so we can get to where we want to go safely; it's an efficient system of free exchange. When the scene in the supermarket is viewed under the aspect of eternity (which the vast scale of Ridley's book tends to suggest), rather than irritation with the mechanics of a chore I feel the wealth of nations being poured out of a mythical and invisible horn of plenty, goods already colorfully stacked and organized in the aisles. How is this not a miracle? And why would one not smile at the people working there who help you with these affordable goods? And, Adam Smith would add, these life-sustaining goods have come into being through individuals acting out of self-interest within a market economy.

So in my opinion it's a wonderful book, a book full of wonders, a comic vision of our prosperity when we look with the eyes (without the overlay of impatience and irritation supplied by the mind's habitual content) to see a wonderland of human ingenuity. Ridley wrote the book hoping to open the eyes of his readers in this way, for then we might be more confident about the world in which we live and the world we will pass on to our children. He acknowledges his son and daughter in the dedication and in the final words of *The Rational Optimist*. This pride of place suggests a more personal reason for the book; as a parent he would be optimistic for them.

The Miracles of Comedy When the Miracles of Science Fall Short

Like *The Rational Optimist*, my first book is about the survival and prosperity of individuals, families, and nations. Unlike Ridley's book, however, *A Comic Vision of Great Constancy* is concerned less with political issues and more with the nihilism I encountered as a teacher of adolescents. Everyman is a philosopher in that everyone has an opinion about life and the world we inhabit. Even though Ridley argues for optimism throughout his book, in the final pages he catalogues the "suffering and scarcity" that feed a pessimistic outlook. As stated in the title, Ridley is a rational optimist, and he persuades his readers to be more optimistic with reasoned and well documented arguments. But what about people who are irrational? What will persuade them to be more optimistic if they aren't particularly interested in economics and politics and don't read books like this one. Furthermore, what about rational, sensible readers who nevertheless suffer from irrational life-style choices, from bouts of depression (even though they live in comfort), or from anger that explodes at any perceived slight. Young people especially still find plenty of evidence in their own lives to support the idea that, as the bumper sticker tells us, "Life sucks and then you die." No wonder. There's a rip tide in youth culture that strongly encourages that attitude. We teach our kids that knowledge is power. But what do we do when the brightness of knowing goes dark, and the mind knows only nihilism, aggression, and despair?

It's difficult to witness how this knowledge (that life sucks, and there's nothing to be done about it) can destroy a young person's will to live. These experiences confronted me with the problem of pessimism at a visceral level. People rightly tout the many miracles of this scientific age, but science has not been able to solve the problem of pessimism scientifically; subjective opinions, even when they are dead wrong or plainly unhelpful (and even if the one who holds them thinks they are wrong or unhelpful), can still rule the lives of human beings.

Since I was a high school English teacher, I found a lifeline in the literature that was my subject. In comedy a character's obsession with a fixed idea makes him and the people around him crazy and miserable. He wants what he doesn't have, and the frustration leads to pessimism. Because an obsession is so narrowing, though, leaving out as it does most of life, life rebels and overwhelms it. The ancients recognized thousands of years ago that people survive and prosper when they can let the idea go, and they called that experience comedy, a lifting up of human beings. The smallness of an obsessive idea in contrast with the greatness of things-as-they-are can be funny once the malignancy has been drained out of it, but the whole process is deeply serious.

For example, in "The Knight's Tale" Duke Theseus stops the young knights Palamon and Arcite from hacking away at each other with swords. Once he has all the facts—including that the woman for whom they are fighting doesn't even know they exist, Theseus transforms their bloody battle in an instant from tragedy to comedy, from a fight to the death to an entertainment by clownish fools. When we share the greatness of Theseus' comic point of view, we can look at the young knights and wonder, "What were they thinking?" It's only a first step in learning to question our own fixed ideas, but at least it's something, an opening in the direction of self-government.

I count it a blessing to have been an English teacher, for I was inclined in that capacity to follow comedy's lead. A deep appreciation for our sentiments, for love, reigns in comedy, and love is a great leveler, a profound common denominator. At the beginning of every school year for twenty-eight years, Chaucer's Theseus opened up a comic worldview to his people and to me and my students:

> *The God of Love! Ah, Benedicte!*
> *How mighty and how great a lord is he!*
> *No obstacles for him make any odds;*
> *His miracles proclaim his power a God's.*
> *Cupid can make of every heart and soul*
> *Just what he pleases, such is his control…*
> *Well, well, try anything once, come hot, come cold!*
> *If we're not foolish young, we're foolish old.*

This is plain speaking easy enough for anyone, from high to low and from young to old, to understand it. Comedy, though, can be entirely non-verbal. What needs to be said as we watch a clown trying for the first time to walk with roller skates on his feet? We laugh at his antics and wordlessly acknowledge the difficulty of balancing what we know (walking) with what we don't know (walking on wheels). By depicting the divine foolishness of love, comedy represents a mirror for self knowledge and opens up a wonderland for civic peace. It's a timeless mission.

The miracles of science are there for all to see. For the most part, though, we take them for granted. To complement and fully appreciate the miracles of science, we need the miracles of comedy, for they open our eyes to life itself as the ultimate and irreplaceable good. Like Atlas hefting the globe it lifts us up, and it's the first stage in becoming an optimist.

Chapter Four:
An Arena for Relationships

Thomas Cole's *Interior of the Colosseum, Rome*

Learning from Old Masters

From 1789 to 1799 the government of France was characterized by mob rule. Perhaps even more than the American War of Independence, these events forever changed the way the world thinks about politics. Because he correctly sensed the importance of the revolution in France, Edmund Burke engaged Thomas Paine in a debate about the meaning of it. Their disagreement has now inspired Yuval Levin to write a book called *The Great Debate* which outlines their arguments.

Just as Thomas Sowell was interested in the way our politics revolves around *A Conflict of Visions*, the title of his book, Levin tells us that he has long been interested in "the sources and the nature of distinct points of view" like those of Paine and Burke. Just as Adam Smith's understanding of "the human heart in conflict with itself" caught Russ Roberts' attention in *The Theory of Moral Sentiments*, the conflict between Paine and Burke intrigued Levin for the way it poses "moral and philosophical questions regarding what each of us takes to be true and important about human life." To make us aware of those questions, Levin has carefully excavated and organized material from Paine's and Burke's books, pamphlets, and correspondence and then illuminated them with insightful commentary. It's a very large undertaking, and consequently *The Great Debate* is not easily summarized. I have read some ridiculous reviews of it that miss almost all of its insights.

To learn as much as I could from their debate, I have attempted a recreation of it. Since I was an English teacher, I did it this sort of thing for thirty years when presenting a lesson on a literary work, and more recently I've written *A Comic Vision of Great Constancy* to recreate "The Knight's Tale" and *A Midsummer Night's Dream* for contemporary readers. I've come to understand this exercise better through an analogy with painting. A student who studies painting in an atelier learns the art of it by copying the works and techniques of old masters. Recently, my wife and I went to a show in the studio of Steve Carpenter, an accomplished local artist. He exhibited a painting there based on a figure by Rubens. When I asked him about it, he explained that it was one in a series of paintings and added that he didn't think he could ever exhaust what Rubens could teach. In the same spirit, Yuval Levin has dedicated himself to copying in a fair hand the work of the old master Edmund Burke so he could thoroughly grasp and communicate Burke's essential insights.

An atelier is not just about a method of instruction; it confirms a worthy goal or purpose. Artists study there to learn how the great masters created beautiful paintings, and in doing so they are acknowledging the existence and importance of beauty in their lives. Burke studied English history to learn how his countrymen have survived and prospered over the centuries, and in doing so he was acknowledging the existence and importance of a moral order in the life of the nation. As a part of the exercise, Levin includes his own insights, drawn from his own time, and this adds another dimension to his recreation of Burke's ideas. I do this as well in my first book and in the essays of this volume. The analogy with an atelier clarifies for me the method and purpose of these writings. Great art and good government are both concerned with transmitting life saving principles. Just as Burke realized the existence of a standard for government in the trials and errors of English history, I would realize the standard (the life saving principle) of an old master's work through my own experience. The discovery of that standard is of great value and its own reward. The saving grace of the process is part and parcel of a comic vision as I understand it.

I have divided the work on *The Great Debate* into four installments. This first essay covers the beginning of the book up through the second chapter called "Nature and History."

A Conflict of Visions

Paine argues in *Common Sense* that his political ideas are grounded in natural rights, the ones enlightened philosophers had finally discovered. Jefferson's Declaration, written in the same year as *Common Sense*, affirms that natural rights are inalienable, and since then Paine's and Jefferson's ideas have become the coin of American political thought. Levin has written his book to rebalance the debate between Paine and Burke. He makes a persuasive case that Burke, like Paine, is an Enlightenment liberal committed to government reforms that are consistent with the liberal goal of freedom for individuals. Given the dominance of Paine's thought in American culture, though, he has a difficult task.

From the complete title of Sowell's book, *A Conflict of Visions: Ideological Origins of Political Struggles,* we learn that he intends to explain why reasonable people can have strong political disagreements. He points out that the conflict about which he writes is rooted in the fact that the two sides have different visions for critical concepts like equality, power, and justice. For example, how can two people act together to ensure equality in society if for one it means the equality of a result—as in the social capital available to each person, and for the other it means the equality of a process—as in each person having the right to a fair trial in a case of law?

Similarly, Levin explains that Paine and Burke have different political philosophies because they define nature differently. For Paine, Levin writes, nature means "the condition that preceded all social and political arrangements." Nature has to be pre-social because Paine believed civilization—prior to the Enlightenment at any rate—had corrupted our natural state. By means of this thought experiment Paine determined that a human being in a state of nature is an individual with natural rights. Burke, on the other hand, sees civilization as a friend of man, not his enemy; there is nothing unnatural about the arts that man has devised to make his life more secure and beautiful. Rather, the changes human beings have made over centuries through trial and error bring us closer to an underlying principle of truth. Human beings and their history are an intrinsic part of a natural whole. The "given world"—the one every generation inherits from the previous generation—is the result of this natural process, and it's a mistake to say that it's unnatural or to undervalue it.

The different definitions of nature lead to different definitions of freedom. Since for Paine human beings "are always most fully understood as distinct and equal individuals," everything in Paine's political philosophy revolves around an individual's freedom to choose the manner in which he will live. Levin explains that for Burke, though, "A government doesn't derive its legitimacy by beginning from proper principles, drawn from nature. Instead, government develops through time along lines that serve the needs and well-being of the people and therefore point toward some natural idea of the good." To define freedom Paine begins with a thought experiment about individuals in a state of nature whereas Burke studies how English civil society keeps people safe and happy as it evolves. More specifically, Burke's nature, which includes established cultures, protects the well-being of the people through stability and continuity. From observations of nature and human history, Burke addresses the question of an individual's freedom. Societies achieve stability and continuity, he argues, when its citizens fulfill their essential human obligations and relations, especially those involving the family. These are not matters of choice. Our freedom flows from meeting obligations, for this is what brings civil peace to a family, a community, and a nation.

This may appear to be an academic argument, but both men believed that these principles governed the lives of people for better or for worse. Because Burke was convinced that Paine's ideas ruled them for worse, he wrote *Reflections on the Revolution in France* to steer the English away from the French experiment with natural rights and mob rule. Following Burke's lead, *The Great Debate* offers insight into what cultivates the discontents that lead to mob rule and into the prescriptions that Burke believed would inoculate a nation from these fevers. Intellectuals beware. It's an intellectual book for sure, but it's Burke's view that some public intellectuals insert "a great danger" into political thought. When politics is reduced to abstract rights and principles, he argues, people's feelings about government are corroded. Intellectuals seduced by the spirit of Enlightenment to devise abstractions about human nature may mean well, but the French revolution proved that their ideas could unleash a terrible violence, the exact opposite of the peace and solidarity they intended.

Because these essays aren't just a copy of Burke's or Levin's ideas, I sometimes add figures of my own to the picture. In the two hundred years since the French Revolution, there have been many experiments to put man in a state of nature; the twentieth century will go down in history as another critical and very deadly phase of them. One of the last, in Cambodia, is a classic for brevity, clarity, and calculated mass murder. The Khmer Rouge systematically ended civilization by moving everyone out of the cities into the countryside where they were reassigned to death or a subsistence way of life. Even though the leaders of the Khmer Rouge advocated a peasant lifestyle for everyone and used peasant soldiers to do their bidding, they themselves weren't peasants or laborers and knew nothing about that life. They were intellectuals educated in France.

Given the importance of intellectuals and experts in the government of modern life, it's clear that Levin shares Burke's concerns about intellectuals and mob rule. Why else would he go to the trouble of reviving Burke's ideas when they were safely buried and forgotten.

A Kind of Choice

A. A Tragic and a Comic Vision

Paine acknowledges the individual's need for society when he writes, "No man is capable of supplying his own wants," but Levin then summarizes the way Paine prioritizes the individual and society in the following sentences: "Human beings are therefore social creatures with needs and wants that reach beyond themselves. But even for the purpose of assessing their sociality, humans are best understood as equal and separate individuals." For a student of literature, the two parts of this statement are constructed around the same tension that gives comedy its motive force. As in Paine's view of human nature, characters in a comedy have consciousness and free will. Since they live in a social context, though, their autonomy proves to be problematic, and it's the business of the comedy to resolve the conflict. In Paine's version, the individual stands alone at the end of his little story, in spite of his social context. In traditional comedy the individual marries and merges into the social fabric.

Paine's stubbornness about our individuality suggests the fatedness and the fixity of characters who are the focus of tragedies. Burke, on the other hand, chooses nature as a model for managing "change, decay, renovation, and progress" rather than a willful, solitary individual. Within the context of an extended family, for example, there's always going to be birth, youth, middle age, old age, and death—all present at the same time; this is true for a species in nature. The appeal to nature, Levin writes, "quite unlike Paine's, does not yield in individualism but in a case for the implicit and inescapable embeddedness of every individual in a larger context." For Paine's individual, the story ends at the end, or as Porky Pig, used to say, "That's all, folks." For the characters in a comedy, there's the stability and continuity of families like that of a species in nature, and that is all.

B. Hands that Express Gratitude For Life

Levin emphasizes that Burke saw his interpretation—our inescapable embeddedness—as a model. For Burke, Levin explains, "This approach to politics is a kind of choice, not a natural fact." By accepting our embeddedness, we express gratitude for the life we have been given. Our acceptance or consent is "a kind of choice." I believe Shakespeare intends to make the same point by ending A *Midsummer Night's Dream* with a narrative where two young lovers, Pyramus and Thisby, have a choice whether to be or not to be. They choose the latter and die by their own hands. The audience is saved for comedy, though, by the fact the two lovers die but only in a play. The actors then get up and finish their entertainment with a dance for the noble audience. It's the miracle of comedy that they can do so, but it's the miracle of life, the poet implies, that, like those actors, we in the audience can get up from our seats and dance out of the theater to live with more gratitude for life and for the social fabric of our life—if we choose.

We don't have to guess at this meaning of Shakespeare's play because

Robin Goodfellow makes it explicit in his epilogue. If we can pardon the actors of this life, he tells us, the actors will mend:

> And, as I am an honest Puck,
> If we have unearned luck
> Now to scape the serpent's tongue,
> We will make amends ere long;
> Else the Puck a liar call.
> So, good night unto you all.
> Give me your hands, if we be friends,
> And Robin shall restore amends.

We have hands with which to take poison or plunge a sword through the heart, and we have hands to speed Robin (and ourselves) out of the theater with a show of appreciation, if we choose. Burke's choice reflects, as the moon reflects the sun, the one that Robin has given us.

A Comic Structure for Relationship

A. What Makes Us Individuals

Literature for thousands of years has addressed the role of an individual within a social context. Chaucer instinctively saw the relationship as a comedy, especially in *The Canterbury Tales*. Because he would depict the world-as-it-is, Chaucer adds another dimension to his portraits of individual human beings than the one dimensional stick figure Paine employs. For Paine, an individual is simply "an individual." By portraying a character within the everyday activities of a social context and by giving us access to his inner life, Chaucer can show us why he acts as an individual in his own interest. Instead of just saying that he is an individual, the narrative structure of the tale as a whole reveals what makes him an individual.

Individuals, as Paine points out, make choices about the way they want to live, but for Chaucer and for Shakespeare after him this will be more true for a person who has earned a comic gravitas in the school of hard knocks. Prior to that, an individual is characterized by choices that furnish and burnish a self brought into being around an obsessive attachment. These choices have far less gravitas. Chaucer never puts it in a sentence like that; he tells stories that convey the idea concretely. Therefore, to convey the idea concretely I present here a summary, as brief as I can make it, of "The Knight's Tale."

Two knights from Thebes, Palamon and Arcite, are captured after a battle, and Duke Theseus of Athens condemns them to life imprisonment in his keep. They are cousins in the royal line of Thebes and are bound to each other by blood and by deep knightly vows. One day, though, first one and then the other glimpses through a narrow window in their cell a beautiful young girl in the garden below, Theseus' sister-in-law Emily. Each young man is stricken with a violent attachment to her image, so in exactly the same moment that they fall in love they each became mortal enemies one to the other in a war to possess her. Where once they worked in concert as blood brothers, they now work for themselves alone. For the reader, though, their love is absurd. They are imprisoned for life, and the girl has no idea they exist.

Their individuality, Chaucer points out, is directly tied to the attachment. It's a chain, a chain reaction, which links their experience to the great chain of being. This chain is a controlling image in Chaucer's poem and a Medieval metaphor for the universe, the whole that's the "larger context" in which there's a time and a place for everything. (For context on "the larger context" please see Levin's quote above about our "embeddedness in a larger context," page 41.) The young men's obsession with the image of the woman motivates them to act for decades in pursuit of her. One of them, Arcite, is released from the prison at the request of Theseus' friend Perotheus. He can leave, but if he ever returns to Athens he will lose his head. Arcite could live freely in Thebes as a royal prince, but he chooses instead to risk his life by returning to Athens where he can serve Emily as her page. The other man, Palamon, also acts on his own behalf. He chooses to escape from prison solely to claim the woman for himself.

These men are nominally free, but they remain slaves to their attachment. In addition to their dodges and escapes, they fight each other all day in the wood to determine who has the right to claim her, they travel all over the world amassing an army of knights to help them fight for her, and once again they fight for her tooth and nail in the tournament Theseus arranges to decide the issue. To establish a judgment that's open to all and final, Theseus designs and builds an arena large enough for everyone in the dukedom to watch Palamon and Arcite fight for their love. None of the lovers' individual acts, however, gains the prize for them. Arcite wins the contest in the arena, but his victory lap proves to be his undoing. His horse suddenly rears up, and the saddle bow crushes his heart.

Everything after the glimpse of Emily is a blur of self-interested activity, and as such the two knights seem like any individual who strives to possess the good life for himself. But they aren't just "individuals." They are individuals with a particular passion. Chaucer has put their desire to possess the image of Emily at the heart of everything they do. Is this a choice? Anyone who has ever loved like this would have to disagree. Desire for the image drives them, and it divides them, that is until Arcite's heart is literally crushed by his saddle bow.

After three days, Arcite realizes that he will not survive the accident, and he calls his cousin and Emily to his bedside. With his last breath, he confesses to her the truth. He knows now, now that he will never possess her, that the attachment is, and always was, essentially empty. He knows now that he has sacrificed the whole world in pursuit of it, and so he lets it go. The emptiness of the image, however, has left a space for a different kind of love which recalls his ties to his cousin, and the nobility of spirit they learned together as children comes back to him. In this spirit he advises Emily to "Forget not Palamon" were she ever to marry. No longer at war with his cousin, he affirms the social context which will be strengthened by the renewal of his knightly vows and by the marriage of Palamon and Emily. So the thrust of the saddle bow ends the obsessive attachment begun by Cupid's bow.

B. Insight into the Way We Love

There's a symmetry to the two bows that's like the symmetry of the angels at either ear of Everyman. The arrows loosed by Cupid's bow produce the attachment to Emily's image. Because of it, the knights become autonomous actors on their own behalf. They would possess her the way a man possesses a woman, but Chaucer knows very well that this instance of a man and woman is simply an archetype for thousands of other attachments that have the same effect, namely the radical narrowing of an individual's consciousness to the task of winning its object. A Medieval Christian would have called the effect *cupiditas* (cupidity) in honor of the winged boy. An individual acting under the influence in this way experiences the autonomy of attachment.

The other bow ends the attachment with a swift sharp stroke like the stroke of death. Nevertheless, after a time to grieve (three days in Arcite's case), the dreamer of the attachment awakens to find himself in a new world that springs to life after the enchantment, a state of being that Medieval Christians called *caritas*. It's a love of the whole from which objects derive, and because the mind is more used to grasping objects, it's difficult to describe. When Arcite awakens to find that the object for which he loved and suffered so deeply was an illusion, he can regard the past and present suffering of his cousin and Emily with compassion. Despite the brutal smarting of his loss, to which he gives voice, we sense a thankfulness that he has lived long enough to love in a new way. The whole experience has a sobering effect. Seeing more clearly what needs to be done and said, he gains the autonomy of wisdom. Even though the two phases of love are divided in an essay like this for the purpose of illustrating their separate dynamics, they are in fact one thing—like a living organism growing to maturity.

C. A Kinder Purpose and a Pleasing Shape for Desire

Can we be wise apart from the experience Chaucer is describing through the character of Arcite? Can we be wise from reading a book or an essay? Can we choose to be wise? People may have an experience like Arcite's but fail to make it a life changing experience. This, I believe, is what Burke means when he writes that benefiting from the experiences of human history including our own history "is a kind of choice." And, we might ask, what role does reason play in it?

A good portion of Levin's chapter on "Nature and History" is taken up with Burke's critique that reason alone does not govern a man. If individuals are not rational, the faith of a thinker like Paine has been misplaced. It's a dangerous error. Since these philosophers underestimate the power of unreason in others (and themselves), it leaves the door open for irrational violence to make its appearance on stage. It's what Burke observed in the French revolution. Levin points out that Burke had always been aware of the role the passions play in human affairs from his first serious work, an essay on aesthetics. Fear of death, for example, "exercises enormous power over the human imagination." These emotions, Burke thought, must be managed by "an appeal to man's simultaneous (if often weaker) attraction to order and social peace." The emotions evoked in relationships with loved ones, friends, colleagues, one's community, and one's nation can also exercise great power over the imagination and the will.

For all its unruliness, emotion naturally binds people together, but it requires a form to weave it constructively and beautifully into the social fabric. We learn from our own experience, from history, and from comedy that, left unchecked, emotions tied to an obsessive attachment can "run away with us." Rather than containing people's emotions with the articulated reasons and the enlightened rule of philosopher kings, Burke favored family life, customs, institutions, courtesy, traditional stories, and common sense as systemic forms of reason. To borrow another expression from popular usage, Burke's model and the form of comedy "fight fire with fire." Even though the burning sharpness of desire can spread like wildfire in a person and burn up everything in its path, human beings discovered over millennia that the pain of desire could be managed and even transformed by those desires which, as Paine puts it, impel a man into society "as naturally as gravitation acts to a center." There's a space and a time within the great chain of being which can give desire a kinder purpose and a pleasing shape. People have found that definition and structure in institutions like marriage, and this is what Burke's model and comedy celebrate.

D. Chaucer's Arena

While comedy establishes a program for civic peace, the program has a strong element of de-programing built into it. To establish that peace, people have to be upended, knocked off their high horse as Arcite was. In a comedy, characters run around like chickens with their heads cut off because they have lost their heads to a fixed idea. A philosopher can be stricken like this as easily as a lover. All men are passionate even if it's only a passionate desire to be "cool," and comedy enjoys showing that, no matter how heatedly philosophers disagree, a great passion will "turn" a lover's reason into passion's devoted servant. Chaucer designed the arena where the two lovers will fight for Emily to acknowledge that passion, like a first born son, comes before reason in the great chain.

The design reflects the three major gods associated with this love triangle. Arcite worships Mars, the god of war; Palamon worships Venus, the goddess of love, and Emily worships Diana, the goddess of chastity and wisdom. If human beings could choose to be wise, then a man in a hurry might fashion himself to others as already perched above the unruly passions of love and hate and able to see what those in the arena of love and hate cannot because they are too embroiled in the conflict. Chaucer's arena, however, is closed to these pretenders, for wisdom accrues from long experience on the floor of the arena itself. People can only enter it through the door in the temple of Love or the door in the temple of Hate. There is no door in Diana's temple. For better or for worse, we express our humanity—we become human—in our passions. Diana's passion to be chaste (or wise) is still a passion. Wisdom and chastity must first enter through the gates of love and hate, carried as a seed in a passionate human being. Desire is our ticket at the gate of Venus while rage is our ticket at the gate of Mars.

Chaucer could have inferred much of this from the story of Esau and Jacob in the Old Testament. Esau, the first born son, is a passionate, impulsive man. In a fit of hunger he gives up his birthright for a bowl of pottage. The blessing goes to Jacob, the clever younger son, but he doesn't gain anything from it just because he's clever. To actually realize the blessing Jacob has to labor many years for it in exile, to wrestle for it all night with an angel, and to reconcile with his brother who wants to kill him. Both narratives confirm that people develop wisdom as they struggle in the arena of love and hate. To reap the fruit of that struggle, we first have to enter the confinement of the arena.

From ancient days family life has served that function; most are born into some form of it. Marriage, too, is an arena for learning "the implicit and inescapable embeddedness of every individual in a larger context." So it is in our jobs and civic life. Experience within the larger context is continually teaching us, if we have eyes and ears with which to learn, that we don't know everything—about the other, about ourselves, or about the world. The lessons or wake-up calls that strengthen relationships are the subject of comedy. It's why we continue study and applaud those works that delight and enlighten us with comic insight.

Chapter Five:

The Art of Self-Government

Ulysses and the Sirens Roman mosaic from Dougga

This is the second installment in a reading of *The Great Debate*. The quotes here come from and the commentary is largely based on the third chapter called "Justice and Order."

The Quest for Home

A. The Nakedness of Odysseus: Lost at Sea and in Bed with Penelope

Thomas Paine built his political philosophy on his idea of man in a state of nature. Within the safe space of a thought experiment, he asserts that "human beings are best understood as equal and separate individuals." Homer includes in *The Odyssey* an incident that conveys an austere sense of man's individuality. It's the tableau I've described previously when Zeus destroys Odysseus' ship, his link to civilization, and the hero finds himself adrift, a naked man in a vast ocean. Unlike Thomas Paine, however, Homer doesn't construct the moral order of his epic on this picture of Odysseus in a state of nature. Instead, the narrative about him is framed from the start by that which motivated him for twenty years—a determination to return to Ithaca and resume his place there with his wife, his son, and the members of his household. We learn about this overriding purpose from a conversation in the opening scene which Athena, the most steadfast advocate for Odysseus among the gods, insists on having with her father. Zeus concludes the meeting by assuring his daughter that Odysseus will make it home to restore order in his kingdom, and he sends Mercury on a mission to ensure that his will is carried out.

The full portrait of Odysseus gives us an impression of a man who could never be an individual in a pre-social state; the influence on him of his social context is too strong. As a naked man in a vast ocean, he's not an individual; he's Nobody. It's why he longs for his place in Ithaca. Odysseus returns to fulfill his obligations there, but a conscious effort plays no role in the final leg of his journey. The Phaeacians sail him to Ithaca sound asleep in the stern of their ship. Once he's there, though, he gets to work. In addition to reestablishing a legitimate government for his people after a twenty year absence, he consents to pay his debt to the gods for the harm suffered by Polyphemus, son of Zeus, as it was Odysseus' reckless overconfidence that trapped him and his men in the one-eyed monster's cave. No wonder his self-opinion was so high when he set out from Troy. Everyone knew him as the great Odysseus, sacker of cities, and that's how he knew himself. His journey home, however, reveals to him his helplessness in the face of divine powers, and he is forced by circumstances to learn self-government. These recognitions make him fit for his true home—the bed (the embeddedness) he built with his own hands as husband and householder before he left to fight overseas. Throughout his journey home, he's determined to reunite with Penelope for a night of love in that bed.

The nakedness of human beings is a leitmotif with which we're quite familiar, but it's a coin with two sides. One bespeaks vulnerability and the other intimacy. Our nakedness as a solitary individual (an ego) shows up in dreams; we see it in a cremation ceremony like that on the Ganges; it's featured in the story of Adam's and Eve's expulsion from Eden; and the thunderbolt of Zeus reduces all the outer layers of Odysseus' life—his ship, his authority, even the clothes on his body—to nothing. From a political point of view, our individuality nowadays is assumed as the given to which our rights are firmly attached. Those rights are a magnificent hedge against our many vulnerabilities and make it easier to agree with Paine's idea of man in a state of nature, for which there is much empirical evidence. After all, babies are delivered naked into the world; we mature as individuals to realize that our minds are fated forever to be subjective centers of consciousness; we survive in the world as individuals by aligning ourselves as best we can with other individuals; and, to emphatically seal the argument, we die alone. We take Paine's point, but the comic vision of Homer, Chaucer, Shakespeare, Adam Smith, and Edmund Burke begs the question as to whether human beings are best understood in this way. If there's a better way, we would be fools not to entertain it.

B. A Standard for Order

I read *The Great Debate* only after *A Comic Vision of Great Constancy* was published. Nevertheless, there are so many correspondences between the two it's as if I had. For example, in the Introduction called "The Business of Comedy" I tell the story of my own encounter with the world as a public school English teacher. It was sink or swim to save my job, for adolescents in groups are experts at exposing the weaknesses of a teacher. Through a painful process of trial and error, gradual change, and constant negotiations with the students, I learned over time what and how to teach. Texts by the old masters, in which I immersed myself as a survival instinct, taught me about self-government and guided my instruction in the art of it. After retirement, I decided to write about the experience, and the book went through a similar process of trial and error over ten years of research, writing, input from editors, and rewriting to realize its present form. I wrote the Introduction to show the reader how the quest for a moral order played a role in my own life, and in essence it's much like the quest for home in *The Odyssey*. Almost six years after writing it, I was pleasantly surprised and encouraged to find that the elements of my story resemble the form of government Edmund Burke calls prescription.

Unlike Paine's emphasis on the individuality of human beings, which is simple and straightforward, prescription is an elusive notion, difficult for a writer to pin down and for someone unacquainted with it to grasp. Levin defines it variously in different sentences and in different contexts, but overall he seemed to be describing something much like comedy. The recognition of my own experience in these descriptions was a confirmation, in a small but important way, that a standard for order, the touchstone of Burke's political philosophy, exists and has always existed. A naked encounter with the world makes me think of Adam and Eve's banishment from Eden. Before they go, however, the Lord clothes them with his own hand, an incident that Chaucer recreates for us when Duke Theseus himself dresses the body of Arcite with his own hands before its cremation. A standard for order, the constant subject of wisdom literature, exists to clothe us in our encounters with the world, and, as the cremation fires along the Granges testify, they include an encounter with death.

C. Comedy As Insight: A Foundation for Getting the Most Out of Life

I started teaching public school in the mid 70s when education was undergoing radical shifts in standards of all kinds, and it was the best of times and the worst of times to be speculating about government in the classroom. Some of the older teachers were still paddling students, and others employed a school-without-walls style of instruction where students initiated their own learning and governed themselves. The dichotomy and dilemma about how to teach ceased to be a problem when I finally settled on what to teach. I have no doubt that the discovery saved my career for a happy ending. My subject, English, includes a great wealth of material (that I doubt can ever be systematically codified), and I chose to teach comic literature. Because the students found something of value in the material, the effort to learn this content governed the class. When Burke writes that following the English model of government "is a kind of choice," he reminds me of my own choice.

A Comic Vision of Great Constancy defines comedy in its broadest, deepest sense. "The Knight's Tale" and *A Midsummer Night's Dream*, which include instances of young adults who die before their time, present a vision that, by being true to life, affirms a life that includes a death. Comedy is a literary form that incorporates change—including the movement of life from generation to generation and from life to death—as a fact of life, and it provides models for how human beings maintain the stability and composure they require in a world where everything, including themselves, is constantly changing. It has survived for hundreds and even thousands of years because it perennially addresses the deepest fears, longings, and questions of Everyman, all with an eye to helping us get the most out of life. It has survived because it teaches us the art of self-government as we explore the scope of our own powers. Burke claims to base his political theories on a model of nature (as discussed in the last essay) as opposed to an abstraction, but he could have said that he based his theories on the model of comedy without it being any less true.

The Great Law

In Paine's vision, an individual and a government are separate entities, and the nature of man determines the nature of the government. It's important to note that Paine's insistence on the sovereignty of individual choice initially made him a libertarian. During the American Revolution he passionately defended the absolute autonomy of individuals. During the course of the French revolution, however, he came to believe, as Rousseau did, that human beings had to be forced to be free; this led him to support the statism of the revolutionary governments. The about-face implies a fundamental instability at the root of his theory about individual choices. How stable can the choices be when, as wisdom literature reveals, they are rooted in passionate, irrational attachments?

Prescription, on the other hand, doesn't concern itself with ideas abstracted from the given world. Instead, it's a form of government which takes the given world as it finds it and strives to improve the social fabric by building on its strengths. As Burke saw it, the people and the institutions that govern them are intimately related. In Levin's interpretation of that view, prescription builds on the best of those institutions "not because our conventional institutions define the standard of their politics, but because the institutions and conventions that have survived answer to that standard." (It has to be "the best" because dictators tend to build on the worst, those institutions that are based on uncivil even violent biases and practices.) Burke's statement checks the quest of intellectuals who insist on identifying the cause of an effect, like deducing which came first, the chicken or the egg. (For a critique of those who insist on a specific cause for a phenomenon, Polonius in Shakespeare's *Hamlet* is the gold standard. The poor man stakes his reputation—and his life, it turns out—on the claim that he has found the cause of Hamlet's madness.)

According to Burke, the standard of our politics is realized not from a specific cause—as determined by a philosopher—but through a process of natural selection. It's incorrect to believe, as many do, that Burke's ideas would slavishly confine a people to the conventions of a status quo. People are free to learn about their own nature and the goodness of a transcendent standard by living and changing within a social context; the standard that survives and that people follow is the one that allows them to survive and prosper. In other words, it's the one that brings them to a comic conclusion. Levin aptly describes this process in a vivid and comprehensive sentence. "The historical experience of social and political life consists in essence of a kind of rubbing up against the principle of natural justice, and the institutions and practices that survive the experience thereby take on something of the shape of those principles, because only those that have this shape do survive." Burke called this "the great law." Unlike an axiom in geometry, it's similar to that which governs the development of an organism. Biology, not logic, is a better frame of reference for understanding these matters. (I'm happy to confess how important literary devices like analogy and metaphor are to the argument.)

Individuals in an Ensemble

A. Consent

Burke refuses to indulge in speculations about origins. These speculations, he concluded, could only be abstractions, and a humane government has to deal with human beings as they are, not as ideals. Returning to Paine's quote at the beginning of the essay, that people are best understood as equal and separate individuals, it has to be said that we are indeed subjective, autonomous beings. It also can be said that this is a fact of life that comedy addresses. From reading Levin's book, I find that Burke's idea of prescription incorporates individuals as links in the great chain of a "constitutional tradition" much like comedy incorporates an individual's autonomy into a social form that maintains and propagates the species. Just as tragedy is subsumed into a broad definition of comedy (in confronting non-being we realize the incalculable value of being), so individuality can be integrated into the social fabric without taking away the attributes of individuality, one's subjectivity and autonomy. This is because in comedy and in Burke's concept of prescription, a character or a citizen in the end *consents* to play the role he has been given in the given world.

There's a moment in *A Midsummer Night's Dream* that dramatizes this. Workingmen of Athens have formed a company to celebrate the marriage of their Duke with a play. Bottom, the egocentric star of Peter Quince's play, wants to play three of the parts himself. After the third attempt to monopolize yet another role, Peter Quince tells him flat out that he can play "no part but Pyramus." Moved by the possibility that Bottom would withdraw altogether from the enterprise, however, Peter Quince resorts to persuading him that, for the good of the play, Bottom "must needs play Pyramus" and not all the other roles. After a pregnant pause when the outcome hangs in the balance, Bottom replies, "Well, I will undertake it." And so he becomes a part of the silly but wildly successful tragicomedy that puts a decisive period at the end of Shakespeare's comedy. To clarify an important difference between consent in this sense and the kind of choice that Paine advocates, Levin writes that, in Burke's view, a healthy politics (and, he might as well have added, a healthy person) "must recognize these obligations and relationships and respond to society as it exists...Meeting obligations is as essential to our happiness and our nature as making choices."

The key word here is "recognize." When we recognize a friend, we don't choose to recognize him. The recognition is complete in itself. Nevertheless, if he doesn't recognize us because we're in a crowd, then we'll have a choice whether to greet him or not. The second part of Levin's statement, therefore, is just as important as the first. Rational people go to work, strive to be good neighbors, pay their bills, pay their taxes, take out the garbage, look after the children, and so on and on; it's common sense to recognize and meet these obligations. If we recognize as well, without necessarily thinking about it, that the peace of mind and the friendships generated by meeting these obligations are essential to our happiness, then we'll do these jobs and greet a friend to engage in the "work" of relationship. This is what happens in the incident with Bottom. Peter Quince and the others in the little company of actors are all Bottom's friends. They have incorporated to entertain Duke Theseus at his wedding. If they succeed, they will all be "made men." Like recognizing a friend in a crowd and greeting him, Bottom recognizes the essence of these relations and consents to his role in them.

B. The Company in which All Are Made Men

The analogy with actors performing a comedy, in which the ensemble as a whole is the star of the show, prepares for the entrance of Equality on the stage as an issue Paine and Burke address in their writings. For Paine, individual choice is the essence of human nature, and individuals institute governments to preserve the fundamental right of individual choice. Since freedom of choice is the right of all human beings, any social condition, any inequality that hinders the natural expression of choice must be removed. These social inequalities, Paine thought, are unnatural; they are unjust. Since the time of Paine's and Burke's debate, Equality has become a celebrity issue throughout the world. It continues to fuel the fires of revolt just as it did in the French Revolution, and from one election cycle to the next candidates running for president carry its colors into battles for the hearts and minds of voters.

Burke, on the other hand, saw that human beings were naturally unequal and that any scheme to make people equal would degenerate into unnatural, uncivil practices just as it did in the French revolution. For Burke, justice means peace and continuity. A just government doesn't seek a massive overhaul. It ensures there's a civic space within which private individuals can play their parts. The previous essay on *The Great Debate* describes Burke's choice of nature as a model for managing "change, decay, renovation, and progress." (Again, please note how important literary devices of analogy and metaphor are to these arguments.) Burke's view of equality also follows the model of nature. He writes, "The inequality which grows out of the nature of things by time, custom, succession, accumulation, permutation, and improvement of property, is much nearer that true equality, which is the foundation of equity and just policy, than any thing which can be contrived by the tricks and devices of human skill." Burke believed that, if this model were allowed to work naturally, it would level the players in it without having to eradicate "all social distinctions or atomizing society into mere disparate individuals," as Levin puts it.

The Athenean mechanicals in *A Midsummer Night's Dream*, who gather to present a play at Duke Theseus' wedding, act out Burke's theme for us. They work at different trades in the marketplace; there's Peter Quince, a carpenter; Nick Bottom a weaver; Francis Flute, a bellows mender; Tom Snout, a tinker; and Snug, a joiner. Also, as actors (and as Peter Quince insisted) they play individual parts. Nevertheless, they all benefit and will be "made men" by the gold Theseus will give them when they succeed as a company. Shakespeare has arranged it so that these diverse mechanicals succeed in entertaining the audience more directly than any of the other actors. By being what they are and not otherwise (they cannot "act"), they are raised into a divine equality by their play, like stars of unequal brightness that make up a constellation in the sky. Or like the Beatles.

Comedy and the Art of Self-Government

Comedy is an art form that for thousands of years has depicted an individual's initiation as a responsible member of society. It's an old, old ritual. Describing it this way, though, doesn't come close to doing it justice. A good performance of a Shakespearean comedy live on stage, creates a comic energy which builds as we near its inexorable conclusion. There have been so many beautiful sounds (for Shakespeare's text is essentially music) and such a variety of actions and emotional reactions to them that we begin to ride the rest of what we see and hear on a wave of emotion. To borrow a word that Burke frequently uses, the whole thing generates a "warmth" in us as our hearts are engaged by everything that has brought us to this moment. We are moved at real weddings for the same reasons. Do we choose to feel this way? This hasn't been my experience. The warmth is who we are, whether we like it or not. We are, willy nilly, involved, and the emotion of the initiation spills out of the play and lifts us into the presence of something great, something constant in the life of human beings that maintains a decent life with others.

Based on my own experience as a young teacher searching for that which would give stability and continuity for civic peace in the classroom and security in my job, and based on the positive response of students and parents when I built my teaching life around the comic vision preserved by the great comic writers of Western literature, I find Burke's ideas credible. "Burke believes," Levin writes, "that the traditions embodied in England's social and political institutions (what he describes as 'the English constitution'), built as they are on the model of natural generation, are the best means available for his countrymen to reach a transcendent standard for government." Government, Burke advises, has to address, has to appeal to the passions of the people, and I learned from my time in the classroom that this is what comedy does.

The great comic literature available to us in English was the "constitution" on which our little society relied as a common basis for civic peace and on which I relied for continuity over the years. The parallel with

Burke's idea is quite exact. This constitution is the best means available for schooling the emotions that are naturally generated when people mix and match with each other socially. Because we are so involved in our passions, the ancients understood that human beings require a structure to help them recognize what can be learned from them. We need the voice of a wise counselor. Comedy provides that structure and embodies that voice. Over time, interactions with hundreds of students opened my eyes to the power of this wisdom, a transcendent standard for government. If it could manifest itself to me, I reasoned, it could do so to anyone.

Shakespeare has given us the character of Bottom to be Everyman's common denominator. He's a hopelessly self-interested character who aspires to being a strongman like Hercules. But once he has to confront the true nature of this self-interest (he discovers he's an ass), he assumes his proper role in the scheme of things and becomes something extraordinary, a hero who has seen wonders. It's in this spirit that he carries the tragic story of Pyramus and Thisby forward into a comic conclusion. Odysseus is also a hero who has seen wonders, and he learned from his encounter with the Cyclops to exercise self-restraint. The picture illustrating this chapter shows that he had his men tie him to the mast before passing the sirens. Circe had warned him about the danger, and he prudently followed her advice. Homer, Shakespeare, and Burke together are inviting us to entertain the notion that life can imitate an art that's deeply rooted in human nature and human experience. They and the tradition they represent are giving us an alternative to mob rule, revolution, and self-slaughter. It's the art of self-government within a great chain of being, and the choice is ours to learn it.

Chapter Six:
Everyday Life

Pieter Bruegel's *The Harvesters*

This is the third essay on *The Great Debate*. It develops themes that were introduced in the other two.

The Work That Binds People Together

A. Self-Restraint in the Presence of a Larger Intelligence

There's a paragraph in Levin's next chapter, called "Choice and Obligation," which has provided the title of this essay and which clarifies Burke's views on choice and consent. The chapter first reviews some of the ground in the debate already covered. Thomas Paine relies on his theory of origins to declare that the social contract is an agreement (a matter which involves a conscious choice) between individuals. Unlike Enlightenment-liberal social theorists, Edmund Burke didn't think the nature of society could be discovered in an exercise like this. Levin's paragraph explains Burke's objections. Instead of proclaiming a universal law, Burke would describe "the essential character of social life." He observes that theorists like Paine, who base their social contract on speculations about origins, tend to "apply their contract only to extreme situations, grounding it in the moment of founding and drawing from it rules for when revolution may be appropriate."

To borrow an analogy from modern aviation, it would appear that Paine's theory is mostly concerned with the takeoff and the landing, usually the most fearful parts of any flight. This approach, Burke writes, "is not very laudable or safe because in general it is not right to turn our duties into doubts." The phrase "duties into doubts" can be understood in two ways. From Paine's point of view, the duty to guarantee everyone's sovereign right to choose this or that should lead to doubts that everyone has that freedom; properly considered, the doubts will then grow to dissatisfaction and even revolution. (Without much trouble the reader can see this pattern in present day American politics.) From Burke's point of view, an abstract, universal law will undermine with doubts our duty to uphold the binding relations in our families and civic institutions, for the universal law regarding individual choice will supersede those relations. This gravely unsettles the social order, something Burke would avoid. (Here, too, without much trouble the reader can see this pattern as the modern state whittles away the power of traditional organizations—like families, churches, and the rule of law—in American life.) Either way, it's an approach that invites second guessing and unrest, and in his own time Burke offers the French Revolution for proof. Opinions about our society and its rules, he writes, "ought not to be in a state of fluctuation, but steady, sure, and resolved." Unlike Paine's contract, which revolves around rights and writes revolution into it as a guarantor of them, "Burke's contract describes the everyday life of his society." Paine would fundamentally transform society with his theory whereas Burke tries to understand and describe what binds it together.

Bruegel's painting illustrates Burke's approach. It depicts the people of a town working to harvest the grain, and the picture shows that the work as a whole, a process that grows into the binding of the sheaves, is what binds them to each other. In Bruegel's art and in comedy everyday life—which because it's so ordinary can seem to be merely a collection of arbitrary or pointless routines—is transformed by means of a comic alchemy into that which has a substantial and timeless value. Some years ago our family went through a difficult period of transition, and we relied for months on several sources of comfort and wisdom to keep up our spirits. My wife cooked creative and delicious meals every night; our golden retriever kept us centered (around him) with his natural vitality, puckish sense of humor, massive presence, and love of life; and not least, the BBC's tapes of Jeeves and Wooster brought us together before bedtime for a happy hour of wonderful wit and farce. Altogether, it was back to basics in the art of keeping the home fires burning. When daunted with uncertainty, we found a way forward through the natural rhythms and energies of family life.

From reading Levin's book, I find that Burke and comedy are engaged in the same enterprise. They describe the everyday lives of ordinary people in a social context, and they outline as well the nature of wisdom, which is a kind of government that helps us to survive and prosper. *The Odyssey* is a form of wisdom literature, and Proverbs 8 has Wisdom herself tell us that "The Lord formed me from the beginning, before he created anything else." For thousands of years human beings have known that the survival and prosperity of a people depend on this wisdom, what Burke also refers to as a transcendent standard for government and prudence. The exercise of an individual's right to choose for himself comes from a completely different understanding than the exercise of prudence. In the one, the individual self has the sovereignty. In the other, the transcendent standard has the sovereignty. The one emphasizes the will (as in Prometheus Unbound and Nietzsche) and features established institutions as a villain. The other emphasizes the self-restraint one experiences in the presence of a larger intelligence and serves to maintain relationships in families, communities, and nations.

B. Is There Choice or Not in Burke's Model of Nature?

How do human beings become wise? What's the path to it? Levin's book, as well as my first essay on it, introduces a wide angle assessment of the question. Paine finds wisdom in Enlightenment philosophies whereas Burke studies history, which is the history of human trials and errors. In that first essay I pose the question as to whether a man can choose to be wise. If you are an enlightenment intellectual who builds a political philosophy based on the centrality of choice in human affairs, then the answer would have to be that, just as we make choices about everything else, we can choose to be wise. We have the example of Enlightenment philosophers for that. Burke asserts, on the other hand, that an appeal to nature "does not yield in individualism but in a case for the implicit and inescapable embeddedness of every individual in a larger context." When we look to nature (which in this context means everyday life) for answers about social order, Burke suggests that nature's (everyday life's) answer doesn't involve individualism.

The "inescapable embeddedness" of individuals in a larger context poses an important and very traditional question about the free will of human beings. How can there be wisdom if people are merely the expressions of a larger context, for wisdom implies an individual consciousness that can choose between what is wise and what is unwise to do? Levin then immediately adds a qualifier: "But Burke also clearly asserts that he sees this interpretation only as a model. This approach to politics is a kind of choice, not a natural fact...The English, Burke argues, choose to adhere to a model of nature—a model of transmission and inheritance that enables gentle, gradual change—for their political life." Paine would appeal to nature for his theory about individual choice, but it would appear that Burke's "kind of choice" transcends nature, for it (he tells us) is not a natural fact.

There's a tension between the assertion of inescapable embeddedness and the "kind of choice" of adhering to a model of nature. Burke would show that the inescapable embeddedness diminishes choice as a realistic basis for a political theory. Human beings don't choose where they are born, and the rest of their life will be a pattern of obligations "not chosen but nevertheless binding," as Levin puts it later. In the previous chapter on "Justice and Order" Levin writes that, according to Burke, a healthy politics "must recognize these obligations and relationships [the embeddedness referred to in the previous quote] and respond to society as it exists...Meeting obligations is as essential to our happiness and our nature as making choices." So for Burke, is there choice or not? The tension described here explains why Levin devotes most of "Choice and Obligation" to work on this question.

C. The Force That Drives Civic Life

In the first part of the chapter, Levin documents problems that Burke associated with democracy, a form of government which is founded in choice. The tyranny of the majority in a democracy, Burke writes, can be an even greater tyranny than that of a monarchy, for the oppression of a minority will be carried on "with much greater fury, than can almost ever be apprehended from the dominion of a single scepter." When oppression is in the name of the people, the government doesn't have to answer for it. In Burke's opinion it's destabilizing for a regime when everything is done in the name of the majority, including revolution. Any government needs the trust of others, and this won't happen if a large minority is being systematically oppressed.

Problems occur in democracies, Burke believed, because a politics of choice has made a fundamental mistake: political and social life begin in essential human relations and obligations, not in individual choices. Burke writes, "The place of every man determines his duty...We have obligations to mankind at large, which are not in consequence of any special voluntary pact...On the contrary, the force of all the pacts which we enter into with any particular person or number of persons amongst mankind, depends upon those prior obligations." So here's the larger context, our embeddedness. Here's "the essential character of social life." A description of social life can't begin and end with the conscious choice of an individual. It has to account for the "force" of the prior obligations we owe simply by being born into a human family and society, the glue that brings and keeps people together. According to Levin, this vision of obligations "not chosen but nevertheless binding forms the very core of Edmund Burke's moral and political philosophy. An enormous portion of Burke's (and the conservative) worldview becomes clearer in light of the importance he places on the basic facts and character of human procreation." The obligations that characterize family life and specifically the attraction of one person for another function as an all important cohesive force at the heart of civic life.

Personal and Literary Illustrations of Burke's Model

A. Relationships Strengthened by the Force of a Wake-Up Call

Too often, though, the force of that attraction can be blunted and buried by numbing routine and the different ways people self-medicate the constant friction of relationships. This is why relationships and the family depend on the all important force of a wake-up call just as much as the initial attraction. As it happens, I begin my book on Chaucer and Shakespeare with my wife's unexpected pregnancy while we were still in graduate school. That was the beginning of my adult life. The child growing in the womb was the father of the man I'd have to be. With the life of a child on the line, I had no more excuses. The force of the experience is still at work with the addition of another generation. So is this force or feeling a choice? Do people choose to feel this way? Again, that's not how I experienced it. It was like a sudden crack overhead which made me stop and wonder, "What was that?" The force of the stopping moved my life in a different direction. It would have to be measured and governed by a new standard.

Summing up Burke's position on this question, Levin writes, "The role of consent in this view of society is secondary at best. Social relations flow out of natural relations, and consent is assumed where it cannot be expressed, not because the individual chooses to accept his obligations, but because the consent of every rational creature is assumed to be in line with 'the predisposed order of things' [Burke's phrase for that new standard by which my life would be measured]." Caring for a baby is what a rational person does. It doesn't reflect the wisdom or the choice of an individual. It reflects the wisdom of the predisposed order of things. Paine thought everything had to be set down in writing and agreed to in contracts between autonomous individuals. Burke relies instead on a transcendent standard of government, which is so self-evident that it doesn't need to be articulated or chosen, to bolster his argument that consent is secondary.

The comic wake-up call—represented in these essays by the crack overhead, the unexpected pregnancy, the thrust of the saddle bow into Arcite's heart, and the cry of a baby—is primary.

B. The Recognition of a Moral Order in Shakespeare and Homer

I have already weighed in on the role of consent. Bottom in *A Midsummer Night's Dream* agrees to "undertake" the role of Pyramus simply because he recognizes that doing so is in line with the predisposed order of things. (See "Consent," pages 55-57.) If the play succeeds, he and his friends are convinced they will all be "made men." It's the first in a series of recognitions that Bottom undergoes. A second occurs when he wakes up to find himself entirely alone in the woods. His friends all ran away when he appeared on stage transformed into an ass. When he wakes in the morning, the actor Bottom recognizes for the first time in his life that he needs an audience in order to be himself. A Bottom falling to the ground (in the death of his character Pyramus) will make no sound if there's no one there to hear it. The third instance follows right after that when he recognizes, even if only faintly, his transformation into an ass during the previous night's adventures. We watch him as he gingerly feels his head to see if large floppy ears are still there. The sum total of all these recognitions is expressed when he recognizes his friends back in Athens with a hearty, "Where are these lads? Where are these hearts?" After his transformation and sudden separation from them, he acknowledges at last that he needs them as much as he always supposed they needed him. Since they are just as glad to see him, the company will now act together as one.

As I have outlined in the Preface, these essays began with a question about that which enables a nation to survive and prosper despite the taxing missteps which mark the lives of human beings, and they argue that the writers featured here present a compelling answer to that question—a comic vision of self-government based on the natural attractions of relationship and the truth rather than a vision based on coercion and deception. Bottom's recognitions sum up the answer. His company provides a model of consensual membership. A recognition of interdependence empowers natural relations. No one forced Bottom into it; it came to him quite naturally. As a variation on a lover's intuitive attraction for another, it's the glue, the force, that brings and keeps people together. Because a recognition is a whole and the recognitions here are mutual, the seeing and the doing are made one flesh in them, and this is how they will be made men.

I'm sensitive to the importance of recognitions from eighteen years of teaching *The Odyssey*, for Homer has made the recognition of Odysseus the standard of an ethical life. Once Odysseus returns, the fate of the other characters depends on whether they "recognize," either in his person or in their continued loyalty to him, the king who has been away for twenty years but who isn't dead yet. Because he represents a moral order instituted by the gods, those who don't recognize him will die, and those who do will live. Argus, Odysseus' hunting dog, has waited by the front door for all of those twenty years, and although he is virtually senseless with old age, he recognizes his master. The perceptual powers of the suitors, on the other hand, fail them. They are predisposed not to recognize the living Odysseus because they have staked everything on the assumption that he is dead, and so they don't.

C. Perception of Everyday Life

These recognitions of interdependence express the essence of what Burke calls prescription. It's inevitable that our perception of everyday objects—the creature comforts of a home; the routines of work, married life, and family; the conveniences of travel and communication; and the protection we enjoy from police and armed services—can become habituated and dull. It's no wonder that I and everyone else will take an American grocery store for granted. For as long as I can remember there have always been well stocked stores near where I lived. At the same time, as I've argued in the essay on *The Rational Optimist*, it's also possible to recognize that this place with so many good things from all over the world (a wild Alaskan salmon that was caught yesterday afternoon and that can be bought in Rochester, NY in time for dinner tonight) is a kind of miracle. Prescription recognizes the miracle, recognizes the social practices that made it possible, and works to safeguard them for future generations. Argus was not fooled by Odysseus' disguise because his blind eyes didn't distract him from the business at hand. In this he's like the blind poet and the statesman who can "see" what dust and dullness have covered up. Because the recognition scenes in *The Odyssey* involve the king, the locus of authority in the land, they represent the uncovering of a transcendent standard for government, transcendent in that the recognition depends on something like a sudden crack overhead that opens the mind and heart. Because of it, a crack or a gap opens in a generally accepted assumption, in this case that the master (the transcendent standard) is dead, to let in a new world.

Even though the story ends unhappily for suitors, who don't recognize the ethical standard in their midst, *The Odyssey* expresses a comic vision. Family members and retainers still loyal to Odysseus help him to defeat the much larger force of the suitors. The recognition of a king who has been gone for twenty years emphasizes the vital importance of everyday perception. We don't have to wait for a crisis in government to find ourselves in a life or death situation. In every moment life demands our full attention, and we may pay a steep price for inattention. Homer's epic as a whole celebrates the perception of things-as-they-are as an ethical standard. When we look with the eyes (as the eyes of Homer and Claude Lorrain teach us), they are objects infused with the light of a profound gratitude for what we have been given. It may well be that the force of Homer's narrative has helped to establish this standard in the hearts and minds of millions. (For "looking with the eyes," see page 9. For Claude Lorrain's light, see the cover.)

D. Recognizing Our Place in the Great Chain of Being

It's a story that has wide application and continues to embody for us the wisdom that helps people to survive and prosper. Over two thousand years after *The Odyssey* was composed, Chaucer added "The Knight's Tale" to the wisdom literature of the West. Like Odysseus, the soldier Duke Theseus undergoes trials that test and expand the scope of his judgment. As a soldier he has to make lightning quick movements in battle based on those of Creon, his opponent. In his capacity as a judge when a case—like the fight between Palamon and Arcite—is brought before him for adjudication, a sound decision will derive from his perception of everything that touches on the case. Because Theseus' decision concerns the warring cities of Thebes and Athens, it involves the welfare of thousands.

Chaucer has made Theseus a worthy model as a leader because he learns from the different trials of his judgment how complex and uncertain the world is and how difficult it is to make judgments about it. Nevertheless, he affirms that it can be done. This experience is the subject of his speech at the end of the tale, and it's a masterpiece that deserves to be better known. As a soldier at the beginning of the tale, Theseus recognizes a pattern in the movements of his enemy Creon and dispatches him with his sword. As a judge (and now a married man) at the end of the tale, he has to recognize (acknowledge) the movements of everything, seen and unseen, and so he begins his speech with these words:

> *The first Great Cause and Mover of all above*
> *When first He made that fairest chain of love,*
> *Great was the consequence and high the intent,*
> *He well knew why He did, and what He meant.*

Theseus' experiences in the tale have taught him that he is not just an isolated individual judging by a book that only he has read. He's a link in a great chain that ties him to all and everything. Perception establishes his link to the great chain, and it's why he can speak to his people of it. As sentient beings, he tells his people, "we discern this order." By virtue of the life we have been given, perception links us to the first great cause and mover of all above. While we are connected to the overall design (for perception proves that we are a part of it), the perception of a human being, he has learned, is painfully limited. Too often we misconceive, misperceive, and make mistakes. Theseus has also learned, however, that there's a spark, a seed of greatness in this constraint. It's the beginning, be it ever so humble, of wisdom, for through it we experience directly the greatness of what we don't know.

Though we are limited in what we can know and have a limited time in which to know it, within this spark or seed grows a sense that life is a gift, a strange and mysterious inheritance that drops on us (or drops us) from out of the unknown. We think we know the full extent of the gift, but in fact it's still wrapped and filled with meaning yet unrealized. This sense comes before all others. Two hundred years later Shakespeare reminds us that, along with life and the perception of what we know in relation with what we don't know, comes another gift:

> This thou perceiv'st, which makes thy love more strong
> To love that well, which thou must leave ere long.

Everyday Life in Civil Society

A. The Tension Between Constraint and Freedom

We didn't choose to have this life; it was given to us. Nevertheless, as Theseus acknowledges later in his speech at the end of "The Knight's Tale," human beings have the power "to abridge" their days. We can choose to be or not to be. True enough, but this brings us back to Burke's statement earlier. It's "a kind of choice" whether we adhere to Paine's philosophical model of man as an individual in a state of nature or to Burke's model of nature as a history of living things changing and being renewed over time. In the book on Chaucer and Shakespeare I see it as a choice whether we view this life as a tragedy or a comedy. We are free to make that choice, but if we choose Burke's model, we are also acknowledging important constraints. For example, Burke crucially acknowledges the limitations of human reason where Paine relies on reason entirely.

Thus we come to the home stretch in the debate between choice and obligation, the individual and society. In Burke's view Paine's social contract is too much concerned with the takeoff and landing of a regime. Burke's English constitution, on the other hand, is about everyday life and strengthening the ties that bind people together in civil society. For Paine, civic institutions like the family create the inequalities that cause so much suffering in society, and he would remove them to put the individual in a more direct relationship with the state. For Burke, civic institutions like the family are the all important buffer between the individual and the state. He concludes that politics, while necessary, is not where life happens (a theme introduced in the essay on Adam Smith). Civic institutions like the family are not just a buffer; they are an enclave within which one can live with a measure of freedom.

If Burke diminishes the importance of choice, does he also deny that people have rights? Having posed the question, Levin lists for us the rights Burke believed we still enjoy even in a political theory that emphasizes obligation. We have a right to a beneficent government, to justice, to property, to inheritance, to the protection and education of children, and to acting freely without restricting others. But he adds one more that may be more controversial: men have a right to a restraint on their passions. Limiting the range of our choices is a right, an advantage. (Odysseus recognized this right when he had his men tie him to the mast.) Society therefore guarantees some liberties and some restraints. After all, this is the way we live every day. For Burke, we learn through everyday experiences how to balance the two.

It's what comedy teaches. In a comedy characters learn there has to be a brake on headlong desire, what I call a wake-up call and what Burke calls "a controlling power upon will and appetite." Over and over we see this at work in comedy. Chaucer constructs "The Knight's Tale" around the cupiditas/caritas theme (which is described in the first of the Burke essays) to show how these ideas play out in a love story. The two lovers' obsessive attachment to the image of Emily would appear to make them men. They act as individuals with courage and conviction, but they are constrained by the fact that a cousin opposes them with all the strength of his courage and conviction. Arctic's last words unties this knot in the social fabric; he gives up his claim to Emily in his last will and testament. Here's what he says to her as she and Palamon attend him:

> O softly take me in your arms, I pray,
> For love of God, and harken what I say.
> I have here with my cousin Palmon,
> Had strife and rancor many a day now gone,
> For love of you, and for my jealousy.
> And may Jove's wisdom touch the soul in me,
> To speak of love and what its service means
> Through all the circumstances and the scenes
> Of life, namely good faith and knightly deed,
> Wisdom, humility and noble breed,
> Honor and truth and openness of heart,
> For, as I hope my soul may have its part
> With Jove, in all the world I know of none
> So worthy to be loved as Palamon,
> Who serves you and will serve you all his life.
> And should you ever choose to be a wife,
> Forget not Palamon, that great-hearted man.

He is free now, he tells Emily, to see how narrowing the obsession has been, and he sees "the larger context," the effects that a royal marriage between the two will have. It will bring the government of Thebes and Athens out of a warlike state and into the loving embrace of a family. Arcite has every confidence in the love that will bind this family together because it's in harmony with "the predisposed order of things" that he recites for them.

There's a significant irony in the cupiditas/caritas device, however, which people miss in everyday life but which Chaucer's tale makes plain. Initially, the obsessive attachment looks like freedom, and the social context looks like constraint. In the end Arctic recognizes that the obsessive attachment is in fact a mortal constraint, and the social context and the timeless values he describes for us at the end, along with Emily's embrace of his mortal remains, represent a resting place for his soul's repose. Along with Chaucer's sense that life in a social context is a mixture of freedom and constraint (and Shakespeare follows in his footsteps by retelling "The Knight's Tale" in *A Midsummer Night's Dream*), this story about love maturing naturally from cupiditas into caritas describes the role sentiments play in social cohesion.

The basic pattern of freedom and constraint, constraint and freedom that we find in Arcite's love structurally holds up and animates everything in the poem. In the passionate affairs of a human being the two together frame a standard for government when all is said and done. We have to have the passion; and we have to go through the trials of passion that precipitate wisdom's wake-up calls. Chaucer is a master at telling this story, and he was Shakespeare's master. And Shakespeare continues to be the master of those who labor to tell the story whether it's in politics, economics, or literature.

B. Final Instructions: Lovers to Bed!

In keeping with the cupiditas/caritas theme (which he borrowed from Chaucer) that expresses the tension between constraint and freedom in Medieval Christian terms, Shakespeare constructed the conclusion of *A Midsummer Night's Dream* around imagery having to do with constraint and freedom, and I'll conclude this essay with examples of it. In his last speech Theseus ends the evening's entertainment by instructing his guests:

The iron tongue of midnight hath told twelve.

Lovers to bed; 'tis almost fairy time.

The heavy, iron tongue of midnight tolls for us all the end of our day. But not if we are lovers, for newlyweds live lightly by a different measure.

After Theseus leaves the stage, Oberon and Titania take his place as the ruling power there. As Theseus did for his court, they have instructions for their fairy trains. These commands have to do with the purpose and the spirit with which they are to do their work:

Through the house give glimmering light
By the dead and drowsy fire.
Every elf and fairy sprite
Hop as light as bird from briar
And this ditty, after me,
Sing and dance it trippingly.

And Titania adds:

First rehearse your song by rote,
To each word a warbling note.
Hand in hand, with fairy grace,
Will we sing, and bless this place.

The fairies will know very well how to work because Oberon and Titania make it like a song and a dance learned by heart.

Oberon and Titania chiefly aim at a lightness of touch in the fairies' government which is made more likely by the rote learning. To give his charges a mental image, Oberon compares that lightness to a bird hopping from a briar. I call on a memory of my own for a mental assist with this image. A neighbor of ours used to throw bird seed into a very large, dense, and prickly bush. When we'd pass this bush at feeding time, it was alive with about a hundred sparrows. The thing was really humming. Along with the sound of it, I loved to watch individual birds as they moved within the dense confines of the structure, hopping from briar to briar, a fluttery miracle of navigation.

So Oberon pictures them working, doing their small jobs with accuracy and speed. Having instructed them, he leaves them with these words:

> *Trip away; make no stay;*
> *Meet me all at break of day.*

Here the constraints of the bush, the confines of the instructions and of the work—where the workers can only "hop"—are completely gone. The instructions followed and the work done, they are free to fly (Oh, the timeless ease and speed of that first line), like an arrow shot into infinite space (an image from earlier in the play), and the night will pass just as quickly.

Chapter Seven:

A Critique of the Way We Love

From Michelangelo's panel of *The Great Flood*

The fourth essay on *The Great Debate* is based on the chapter called "Reason and Prescription."

What Happens When Metaphysics Is Applied to Politics

It's obvious from the time and effort required to explain and illustrate Burke's point of view that it doesn't lend itself to a catch phrase on a bumper sticker. Paine's argument about choice, on the other hand, is straightforward, and its simplicity gives Paine a significant advantage in political arguments. The word "choice" is enough to sell it. For a modern audience, the word "obligation" requires considerable context and interpretation to make it a selling point. To do justice to Burke's observations, Levin looks at them from slightly different angles as the book progresses. For example, the chapter on "Choice and Obligation," the subject of the last essay, develops the argument which Levin introduced earlier that Burke's approach to politics was "a kind of choice, not a natural fact." Likewise, the chapter on "Reason and Prescription," the subject of this essay, develops Paine's assertion, recorded in "Nature and History," that his political ideas are grounded in rational truths about human nature, the ones enlightened philosophers of his century had finally discovered.

"Reason and Prescription" begins with Burke's observation that an appeal to metaphysics inserts a great danger into politics, and his argument has three specific critiques. First, abstract reasoning about politics, he maintains, confuses people about the purpose of politics. For Burke, government preserves the safety and well-being of the people. When metaphysics enters the equation, government serves to prove a point instead and provides a very large and public forum for the self-congratulation of the social theorist. Abstract reasoning about "rights" in modern politics is a case in point. For example, the supporters of the Affordable Care Act wanted a law to insure people's right to health care. It's a straightforward argument, but the definition and limiting of a right is essentially a metaphysical question. There are an infinite number of potential rights that people might like for themselves, and there's no way to prove empirically or deductively what's an allowable right and what isn't. (It's relevant to this argument that the health care bill itself ran into great difficulty over what medical condition would be insured and what wouldn't. How can it be determined authoritatively which diseases have "rights"? The right to an abortion is still the most controversial part of the health care debate. It continues to be the Gordian knot of our politics because it involves metaphysical questions about the beginning of life and the nature of personhood.)

Given this difficulty with rights, it would be more accurate to say that the supporters of the bill wanted to prove that the right to health care existed by making it a law. Jonathan Gruber, the MIT professor who claimed to be a lead designer of the Affordable Care Act, boasted to friendly audiences that the law's abstract, arcane complexity was deliberate. It's what enabled it to be passed. Because it was impossible for the average voter and the average elected official to understand it, the public bowed to the superior intelligence of the expert, intellectual designer. Does the bill serve the safety and well being of the people? Its supporters may have thought that it would, but apparently that was a secondary issue. Otherwise, they would have written a simpler and less controversial bill. The bill's supporters wanted to win a longstanding argument with a decisive overhaul of the system. (The politics of the health care law is my example, not Levin's.)

Second, if government has become an academic argument, those who are promoting a theory will tend to ignore (or eliminate) circumstances, the details that make up a complex social order. It's the nature of argument. To illustrate this point, Burke observed that the radicals of France divided the country up into districts that were perfect squares. On paper it looked like a rational arrangement, but it completely disregarded the long history in France of distinct regions with their own languages and cultures. Geometry eliminated the social realities that previously bound the people of a region together. This is a technique of social engineering that the leaders of the Khmer Rouge learned when they studied in France. Back in Cambodia, they uprooted the people from their traditional homes and roles and forced them into abstract "collectives" that the state defined. It's the technique Stalin employed when he moved as many as 100 million people out of their homelands to work in Siberian collectives. Stalin had a theory about collectives, and independent farmers who didn't do what they were told had proven to be an obstacle. Out of respect for the theory and to solve his problem with a group that didn't fit into it, he dislocated or killed a whole class of people. They were the "circumstances" of which he rid himself. Then, too, Hitler had his theory about and final solution for the Jews. Burke identified this side effect in the French political experiment, and the dictators of the 20th Century have provided massive proofs of it. (The last three are my examples, not Levin's.)

Third, reductive policies encourage extremism. Because a radical government is more about a theory than the safety and health of the people, and because that government has become a form of self-gratification for its theorists, there's no logical limit to implementing the theory. Nothing but total success is acceptable, and the need for it unleashes a flood of unreason. During a trip to Berlin we visited the area around the Brandenburg Gate, the political heart of the country. After the trip, I read a book about the final months of the Nazi regime, which ended with the encirclement of the Reich Chancellery. For many months it was obvious to the Nazi leadership that the situation was hopeless; they had lost the war. Because nothing but total success was acceptable, however, Hitler willfully spent as much German blood and treasure as he could in the death throes of his regime. As the war went against him, he blamed the German people for the failure of his ideology, and he punished them without compunction by declaring a state of total war.

I've used examples from 20th Century totalitarian regimes because Burke's critiques go a long way towards explaining the rotten something that made them failed states in the end. Of course, the theories about race and class inserted more than a danger; they perpetrated the murders of millions in industrial scale genocide and social engineering. Burke understood from studying the French Revolution that mobs don't just happen. They need a metaphysical idea around which feelings can coalesce and a fiery ideologue around whom the people can rally. Levin has written *The Great Debate*, I believe, because Burke's observations deserve more credit for the way they foresaw the fatal path of 20th Century politics. Let us pray we can yet learn something from the mind numbing waste of human life that it produced.

The Nature of Cupiditas

These essays maintain that Burke was drawing on what he called "the English constitution" for his observations and that this constitution includes the literature of Homer, Chaucer, and Shakespeare. We learn much from them about obsessive attachments. In love with an image of total success, activists will pursue an image with the same single-mindedness that the suitors pursued Penelope in *The Odyssey*, Palamon and Arcite pursued Emily in "The Knight's Tale," and Iago pursued the destruction of Othello. The single-mindedness is like the trance into which Narcissus fell when he saw his own image in the pool. Just as an electrical current can't self-correct a short circuit, nothing can stop this path of least resistance until it has spent itself.

Activists of any age spend themselves in this kind of trance, but they still have sense and motion for that which threatens the attachment. No matter how powerful, leaders and members of ideological movements are brutally paranoid. The insights of Chaucer and Shakespeare illustrate that the obsessive single-mindedness and the aggressive paranoia are expressions or manifestations of the way we love. These essays also argue that our classical and Christian culture, preserved for us in the writings of Homer, Chaucer, and Shakespeare, had more insight into this problem than modern politics does. The extreme violence and wreckage of the twentieth century is proof positive that something is amiss, and the social tensions of the twenty-first century are asking questions that a politics based on abstract rights and ideologies will not be able to answer.

Burke's observations and the way Chaucer and Shakespeare frame the question help to explain why the actions of a person or a mob moved by an obsessive attachment to a theory have no natural stopping point—why an Othello violently ignores the truth to kill the woman he loves; a terrorist blows himself up to kill an enemy; a mob burns down its own neighborhood; and young people—who have benefited greatly from the security, the education, and all the comforts of a good home—work tirelessly and sometimes violently to pull down the society that brought them into being. In addition to an obsessive single-mindedness, cupiditas will always involve a rival or an obstacle, for that is the nature of cupiditas. It wants what it doesn't have so it hates the obstruction. Those who love in this way find themselves in Theseus' arena which lets people in only through the gates of love and hate. They are, in fact, the same gate, the one that admits a love/hate relationship. Once inside, they have to fight their rival for the object of their attachment.

Unfortunately, it's a great and dangerous knot in human relationships that the role of rival and object of attachment will often enough be played by the same person. Once upon a time Arcite fought Palamon for Emily. Let's suppose Arcite lived, and he married Emily. If they are like most couples, some time later they'll be back in the arena of love and hate again, only this time Emily will have come down from the stands to fight with her husband. (Chaucer includes the Wife of Bath in *The Canterbury Tales* to tell this story.) Arcite will then fight Emily, the object of his love, for the image he had of his love, and Emily will fight him for the image she had of her love. Shakespeare begins *A Midsummer Night's Dream* with Theseus and Hippolyta, who will be married in four nights, arguing over the character of the moon. It's a quarrel deeply rooted in the self images of men and women. Act II begins with Oberon and Titania, passionate lovers who have been married since time began, bitterly fighting to possess a child they both love. Obsessed with possessing the child, the king and queen of fairyland forget their primary purpose which is the regulation of nature. Because of their brawls, the land is flooded, the seasons alter, and crops and animals die. Oberon and Titania are like of the Ma and Pa of our political system, the two parties that passionately quarrel over the welfare of their people. The stories of Chaucer and Shakespeare help us to understand how a family can become a house divided. It has to do with the way people love.

It explains why survivalists in love with extreme individualism insulate themselves with the dream of living out their days in the wild or a bunker and why the idea is so destructive. If one agrees with Adam Smith, that man naturally desires, not only to be loved, but to be lovely, then the survivalist project goes against human nature, or it's merely a pose. Leaders of North Korea pride themselves on a bunker mentality, but it's well known their independence is a sham. No country can isolate itself from the rest of the world, and extreme individualists depend on the zombies—all of us who live in a social structure—as their reason for being. People continue to love their picture of the ideas in theory even though they don't work out in practice. It's so much easier to love the virtual reality, but there's no virtue (strength or manliness, from the Latin word for "man") in it.

Also, it's a matter of record, as I've mentioned, that Paine's libertarianism evolved during the French revolution into its exact opposite, Rousseau's doctrine that people had to be forced to be free. It suggests that an extreme individualism can lead to a movement that is dominated and led by charismatic leaders or elites who know what's good for everyone else. Those of us who went to college in the 60s remember the long hair, the fight against the establishment, and men like Abby Hoffman who led his Yippies against the aggression and conformity symbolized by the military. Why is it, though, that people who advocate non-conformity so often end up conforming—in the way they dress, act, and speak—to the expectations of their group? It's not just the influence of Rock and Roll, Ayn Rand, talk radio, or the Renaissance Fairs, restaurants, boutiques, farms, and farm markets of free spirits. It's not just about policy and politics; it's about the love of a certain identity and group solidarity.

Comedy as a literary form came into being because the ancients understood that without insight into the way we love relationships die. Without insight into the way we love people around the world suffer from a plague of sentiments gone awry; it explains as cogently as any analysis the rise of domestic violence—in families, inner cities, and civil wars (a titled king of oxymorons).

The North and South Poles of How and How Not to Govern

Burke mistrusted irrational enthusiasm, but he argued as well that reason is an imperfect means of understanding. It reflects the imperfect human beings who employ it. "It is true indeed that enthusiasm often misleads us," Burke writes, but "so does reason too." A government built on proper principles, radicals think, will never need to deviate from them. More importantly, they believe that the government built on proper principles will never fail. Once the regime is in place, time will stop; it's the end of history. But time marches on. Hitler's thousand year Reich lasted for less than fifteen years. The USSR has withered away.

Burke supported the English constitution because he thought it was better equipped to deal with change. Since reason is inadequate as an organizing principle, he looked to prescription as a critique of speculative politics, as a way of emphasizing the "given world," and as an accurate portrait of human nature. That portrait is characterized by our sentimental attachments and by the limits of our reason. Burke strove, as comedy does, to view his people in a positive light. He encouraged them to believe they could meet the challenges they face. Their moxie was a gift of the English constitution which had sustained them over the centuries and which could be relied on to do so still.

Chaucer is an important part of the English constitution in that he puts English moxie into timeless poetry. Though born into a middle class family, he served as a page in the household of John of Gaunt, the most powerful man in the kingdom, and he continued to work in royal households for the rest of his life. His duties included diplomatic missions for the crown to the continent, and in England he worked with people at all levels of society as a tax collector, a master of the works for royal properties, and a justice of the peace. He was one of the most learned authors to write in English as well as an acute observer of men and manners. *The Canterbury Tales* represents a lifetime of reflection on the human condition and on a government adequate to that condition. He gives "The Knight's Tale" pride of place in the collection and writes it in a high style. It must be that he valued it as that which was most worthy of these studies.

He begins the tale with a sharp contrast between two rulers, Theseus and Creon, and he intends them to be the north and south poles of how and how not to govern. As heads of state the success or failure of their governments is reflected in their success or failure in governing themselves, and the success or failure of their self-government is intimately related to their insight (or lack of it) into the way they love. By the end of the tale Duke Theseus has proven himself to be a good man and a good ruler, as I have briefly mentioned in these essays. He succeeds because he demonstrates throughout the tale that he's capable of questioning his own ideas. We never meet Creon himself; we only know what he did, which is enough. The wife of King Capaneus tells the story of how she and the other ladies with her lost their husbands in a siege of Thebes:

> *Now old King Creon—O alas, alas—*
> *The Lord of Thebes, grown cruel in his age*
> *And filled with foul iniquity and rage,*
> *For tyranny and spite as I have said*
> *Does outrage on the bodies of our dead,*
> *On all our husbands, for when they were slain*
> *Their bodies were dragged out onto the plain*
> *Into a heap, and there, as we have learnt,*
> *They neither may have burial nor be burnt,*
> *But he makes dogs devour them in scorn.*

Please note. Creon or his army kills them in a siege. Fair enough. The king commits a crime against nature, however, by not burying them.

Burial of the dead is one of the oldest rituals, customs, or laws known to human kind, and yet Creon refuses to do it. His enemies no longer threaten him so we wonder why he troubles himself about them at all. It would have been easier to bury them than to devote men and resources to make sure they were not buried. It can only be that Creon has an idea about the matter that outweighs the usual procedures and considerations. Since he's the king, it must be a matter of policy, a political theory. We are given no explanation for the policy from the widow's report, but this helps to make Chaucer's point. Without any kind of motive given, we are left with the "tyranny and spite" of it. He is doing it because he can, and nothing but the total success of his idea is acceptable, even if it makes no sense. It's a pristine political theory that springs from one who thinks for himself about these matters and who loves his idea. From Burke's point of view, Creon is the anti-hero of government, the one with no feeling at all for the importance of prescription. Theseus, on the other hand, grasps the significance of the situation immediately. He instantly changes direction and marches through the night to checkmate the man who would do this. We have to assume that Creon has committed a serious crime from the way the woman describes it and from Theseus' response. Crean owns what he did because it's just not done.

Our Freedom Lies in Recognizing the Way We Love

When he was living above one of the gates into the city of London, Chaucer might have seen during a time of unrest a great mob of peasants pouring through the gate on their way to burn down royal buildings. These things, he knew, didn't just happen. As his stories show over and over, human beings are moved by ideas and images. In Chaucer's day, a theorist and innovator like Creon was an outsider, a tyrant; no good could come from a man who left the bodies of the dead unburied. Six hundred years later it's safe to say that most people would share that sentiment.

The problem persists, though, of leaders who would constrain the people through force into a social construct. Creon, the man who defied a custom honored throughout human history to assert a policy answerable only to his own reasons (which reasons, we can be sure, are rooted in an infatuation with an obsessive idea and not the people's health and safety), might have been gratified to know that many centuries later men like himself rose to rule millions even if only for a few years. This happened over a half century ago, and human beings generally retain a sense that no good can come from a man like Creon. Nevertheless, people still have a hard time recognizing a Creon when they see one in the initial phases of his career. Unfortunately, people have trouble even after that when the true colors of his tyranny begin to show.

It would appear to be a perennial, perpetual problem. Like Burke's exhortations, a comic vision encourages us to believe that the problem isn't in our stars; we are not the slaves of fate. Our freedom lives in recognizing the way we love, for worse and for better. It's what saves a lover for a comic ending. As it is for an individual, so it is for the nation. In a comic vision our individual actions, though infinitesimally small in the overall scheme of things, make a difference in the aggregate. We all have a hand in the invisible hand that creates a civil society. In recognizing the way we love, it's easier to pardon—for pardonable offenses—the actors of this life including ourselves. And if we do, we will mend.

Chapter Eight:
The Stairway Up
That Was Never Lost

M.C. Escher's *Relativity*

The Hope for Modern Times

A. A New Man for the Age of Politics

Every page of *Modern Times* by Paul Johnson is dense with well documented details. The effect can be overwhelming if the reader loses sight of the thesis that he presents in the first chapter. The modern world began, he writes, with Einstein's Special Theory of Relativity which "dethroned" absolute time and absolute length. For the general public it was as if the globe had been cast adrift "in a universe which no longer conformed to accustomed standards of measurement." People understood this to mean "that there were no more absolutes: of time and space, of good and evil, of knowledge, above all of value."

Einstein was appalled as, over the next thirty years, "he lived to see moral relativism, to him a disease, become a social pandemic." For Johnson this illustrates "the dual impact of great scientific innovators on mankind." Their genius can change the physical world, but they also can change our ideas. For example, Galileo's experiments led to the scientific and industrial revolutions; Newton's ideas were the inspiration of the Enlightenment which, in turn, inspired revolutionary politics; in the popular mind, Darwin's theory of natural selection became the social Darwinism which justified the racial philosophies of Hitler and others. If it's true that the public understanding of relativity acted like a knife "to cut society adrift from its traditional moorings in the faith and morals of Judeo-Christian culture" as Johnson claims, it explains why Einstein near the end of his life wished he had been a simple watchmaker.

As Johnson does periodically throughout the book, on its last pages he returns to this theme, the vacuum created by the loss of traditional standards and the potent brew with which modern times has tried to fill it. He reminds us that it was Rousseau who argued that "human beings could be transformed for the better by the political process." Rousseau believed that the state, run by enlightened men like himself, would create "a new man." This new man (and many in the 20th Century like Lenin, Pol Pot, Stalin, and Mao Tse-tung saw themselves as exemplars and creators of such men) thought that politics "was the one legitimate form of moral activity, the only sure means of improving humanity." By telling the story of modern times, Johnson demonstrates in exhaustive detail that these new men have deposed the Age of Religion and replaced it with the Age of Politics. In place of religious belief they instituted a secular ideology and a government run by "gangster statesmen." The arrogance of titled lords and monarchs, the bane of Thomas Paine's existence when he wrote his first books, was replaced with "the arrogance of intellectuals" who propagate and police the ideologies.

B. An Opening to Freedom

The story of modern times is a dismal tale. Nevertheless, Johnson has structured his book as a comedy. We begin in the darkness and confusion of The Great War and the destruction of the 19th Century's philosophy of personal responsibility. We move on from there to suffer the "High Noon of Aggression" and the mass murders of World War II, the "Peace by Terror" of the Cold War, all the failed experiments in government of the developing world, and "America's Suicide Attempt" during the 70s. Despite the tragic failures of this Age of Politics, Johnson supplies a comic ending with a concluding chapter on "The Recovery of Freedom" in the 80s. This part of the story culminates in the fall of the Berlin Wall, the exit of Eastern European countries from Soviet control, and the breakup of the Soviet Union itself shortly after that. Johnson writes that this victory "was essentially the work of outstanding popular leaders, who mirrored the thoughts, desires and faith of ordinary men and women. It was certainly not the work of the intelligentsia, philosophers, economists and political theorists, or of academics generally. The universities had little or nothing to do with it, just as they played virtually no part in the first Industrial Revolution of the late eighteenth century." The role of intellectuals, or in this case the lack of a role, is an important theme in Johnson's narrative of modern times.

Comedy, as I define it, is about ordinary people who discover that a closely held idea is just an image or an idea, not reality, and this is the story that Johnson tells. People in the Age of Politics fell in love with the idea that politics was the only sure means of improving humanity. In Johnson's telling of the story, the people of modern times, the main characters, awoke at the end of the century from the enchantment of that idea, and a wave of freedom washed over the entire world as dictator after dictator fell and were replaced with governments that aspired to individual freedom, personal responsibility, the rule of law, democracy, and free markets.

C. An Open Question

Because he last updated an edition of his book in the 90s, Johnson leaves it an open question whether the recovery of freedom would continue. "On that," he writes, "would depend the chances of the twenty-first century becoming, by contrast, an age of hope for mankind." As it happens, he had good reason for doubt. Since the 90s gangster statesmen like Vladimir Putin have returned in force, and the poor economies and weakened national identities of European democracies have exposed them to aggressive actors. As it was in the 70s, America is divided about its destiny as a nation. A mighty tide is now washing the politicians and the public away from its founding documents and toward the democratic socialism (Milton Friedman argues that these are mutually exclusive terms) popular in Europe. Many thought that the fall of the Wall and the breakup of the Soviet Union had decisively ended the debate in favor of individual freedom and personal responsibility, but the enchantment of collectivist ideas would appear to have a perennial staying power.

In *A Comic Vision of Great Constancy* and in these essays I have argued that the fault doesn't lie necessarily in our politics that we are underlings, the captives of an ideology. The last essay affirms that our freedom lives in recognizing the way we love. No matter what kind of government rules the day, human beings are free to love one way or the other. Do we attach ourselves to an idea or image that's a projection of ourselves as Narcissus does, or do we grow—like a plant prompted out of winter darkness by spring rains to take in all the elements of sun, rain, earth, air, as well as "the thousand natural shocks that flesh is heir to"—and live in the open as an expression of life itself.

This last is the image with which Chaucer begins *The Canterbury Tales*. In comedy and in other forms of wisdom literature, human freedom begins, not in politics, but in the human heart. That freedom is the lever, the power of a root to overthrow the pavement, with which individuals can move the world.

D. The Rule of Wisdom

For Johnson, as for comedy, freedom begins in poetry and in a basic recognition of the way things are. An epigraph at the beginning of his book from Psalms, 2: 9-10 asserts the rule of wisdom on earth:

> *Thou shalt break them with a rod of iron;*
> *thou shalt dash them in pieces like a potter's vessel.*
> *Be wise now therefore, O ye kings:*
> *Be instructed, ye judges of the earth*

The breaking and the dashing describes the wake-up call that's the catalyst of a comic vision. The heart and mind of the king who thinks he can rule the people any way he sees fit need instruction, and such a rule will continually chafe the heart and mind of the one who passively submits to it. The quote makes it clear that the king's idea is not reality; the poet is not just imagining this. There's a law greater than the king's that still governs the hearts and minds of every man and woman on earth, and this will always be true.

Burke called it a transcendent standard for government, and I have referred to it as wisdom or insight. We learn about its power when a regime (the world one has constructed around an idea) falls to earth and smashes into pieces like a potter's vessel. Also, we learn in the end not to distinguish ordinary people like ourselves from kings. Everyman is a king and a judge in that, for good and evil, he has tremendous power to shape the world in which he lives. To avoid dashing ourselves to pieces, we, too, can be instructed by the voice of wisdom to learn from our own experiences. A comic vision supplies the hope on which Johnson tells us the destiny of the twenty-first century depends.

The Gnosticism of Modern Times

In Johnson's telling of the story, moral relativism got a big boost in the popular mind from another innovator but one who is neither great nor scientific. Sigmund Freud had been a well known figure in his speciality before the war, but his work in 1920 on a commission investigating therapies for shell-shocked soldiers provided a breakthrough. It led to his discovery by artists and intellectuals. Unlike Einstein, who insisted on the empirical testing of his theories, Freud's theories were "all-embracing and difficult to test at all." According to Johnson, "when evidence did turn up which appeared to refute them, he modified the theories to accommodate it. Thus the Freudian corpus of belief was subject to continual expansion and osmosis, like a religious system in its formative period." His theories gained enough momentum, though, that they became their own reason for being, quite apart from the human health that was supposedly its object. The point, the truth of the enterprise was lost, and this led to bitter factions within the movement. Former colleagues in Freud's circle, like Jung, were treated like heretics when they no longer agreed with him. Freud thought that colleagues who offered resistance were mental defectives. Johnson points out that this attitude "was to blossom in the Soviet Union into a new form of political repression."

Freud succeeded because his work "had literary and imaginative qualities of a high order;" this won him prizes and a wider audience. As his audience expanded, he "allowed his ideas to embrace an ever-widening field of human activity and experience." I've included these details of

Johnson's little biography as a prologue for the introduction of an important theme in Johnson's assessment of modern times:

Freud was a gnostic. He believed in the existence of a hidden structure of knowledge which, by using the techniques he was devising, could be discerned beneath the surface of things. The dream was his starting point. It was not, he wrote, "differently constructed from the neurotic symptom. Like the latter, it may seem strange and senseless, but when it is examined by means of a technique which differs slightly from the free association method used in psychoanalysis, one gets from its manifest content its hidden meaning, or latent thought.

Gnosticism is a very large subject. For the purpose of this essay, I'll simply relate the use that Johnson makes of it. Modern intellectuals—the ones who invent, propagate, and police the ideologies that have replaced religion as a cohesive force in society—play a leading role in Johnson's story, and gnosticism, he writes, "has always appealed to intellectuals. Freud offered a particularly succulent variety." He persuaded his patients and his readers that he had a way to decode the hidden meaning of everyday experience.

Johnson compares his decoder to a bubbly, erotic cocktail that induces truth-telling, the perfect drink for the roaring twenties:

The meaning of dreams, the function of myth—into this potent brew Freud stirred an all-pervading potion of sex, which he found at the root of almost all forms of human behavior. The war had loosened tongues over sex; the immediate post-war period saw the habit of sexual discussion carried into print. Freud's time had come.

For Johnson Freud is a prophet of modern times, and his technique of free association, the content of which is interpreted by an all powerful doctor in love with an esoteric theory, represents its moral center.

I grew up after the war when psychoanalysis was all the rage, and Freud's ideas were a potent influence. From a child's perspective, it appeared that Freud had unearthed or invented for the first time the natural laws of the human psyche. So when the great doctor told us that sex was at the root of everything, who were we to argue with him. Besides, Johnson makes it clear that Freud wasn't the only one interested in hidden sexual meanings. The writings of Proust and Joyce, he tells us, are vast experiments in "subterranean sexual emotions." The novels of the 19th Century taught that "each of us is individually accountable for our actions—which was the joint heritage of Judeo-Christianity and the classical world," but twentieth century intellectuals, artists, and writers changed all that. They imagine a world in which there's a "contemptuous lack of concern for moral balance-striking and verdicts. The exercise of individual free will ceased to be the supremely interesting feature of human behavior." As a graduate student and a young teacher of English, I fell under the influence of this modern point of view without seriously considering its implications. Experiences of time and circumstance, though, gradually de-magnetized its power. From teaching Homer, Chaucer, and Shakespeare year after year in the classroom and from experiences of family life, I was instinctively drawn to their comic vision and repelled by the pessimism of modern literature.

A Government of Gnostic Experts

Johnson maintains that the cultural and political strands of change cannot be separated, so this foray into psychology and art has been a prologue for the entrance on stage of the ideology that occupies so much territory in the story of modern times. Marxism, writes Johnson, "was another form of gnosticism claiming to peer through the empirical veneer of things to the hidden truth beneath." In words much like those of Freud in the quote earlier, Marx had pronounced that, "The final pattern of economic relationships as seen on the surface…is very different from, and indeed quite the reverse of, their inner but concealed essential pattern." The masses were "imprisoned in structures: twentieth century man in bourgeois structures." Because these hidden structures were at "the root of human behavior," the exercise of free will ceased to be a viable concept for

Marx as well as Freud. The actions of human beings were determined by the subconscious or by the place they occupied in the economy. With their freedom of inquiry and action lost, people depended for their mental health on the ministrations of a doctor who understood the secret codes of the psyche, and the masses depended for their economic health on the elite knowers, the disciples of Marx, who understood the secret laws of class and production.

Marx's theories have proved to have many lives. When his prediction about the socialist paradise didn't come true and the Russian revolution turned into a totalitarian regime, his disciples in the Frankfort School infused psychology, anthropology, philosophy, and science with the Marxist idea that the lumpenproletariat was imprisoned in a false consciousness. These intellectual tools explained why the socialist paradise failed to materialize. A capitalist economy wasn't the only barrier; the bourgeois culture would keep capitalism in power and the people in chains for as long as that culture was in place. The Frankfort School was founded, therefore, to fundamentally transform the traditional Western values maintained by Christianity and liberal democracies. An era of personal responsibility and private property would have to make way for a culture that facilitated collective action.

When Stalin's mass murders discredited the whole communist project to the point where even the Soviet government had to reject him, the emphasis on culture in the war against capitalism was renewed by French intellectuals after the student revolts in 1968. These writers, Johnson explains, were "influenced by Marxist determinism, which denies any importance to the individual or to free will or to moral conscience in shaping the world." They came from different disciplines, but they all were seeking "the inner but concealed essential pattern" of culture that kept the socialist paradise from being realized. Even as capitalism lifted rich and poor alike out of material poverty, as it was doing in the developed world where capitalism was deeply rooted, they maintained that Man was still imprisoned in bourgeois structures. Structuralists "dismissed narrative as superficial and individuals as unimportant and preached a doctrine of geographical and economic determinism in history, whose long-term course was decided wholly by such structures." According to the psychologist Lacan, the literary critic Barthes, and the linguist Chomsky, deep structures in social conventions and language overwhelmed human agency, the individual's power to choose. In Johnson's reading of modern times, structuralists are gnostics, an elite group of intellectuals who have been initiated into the hidden patterns of the social order. These groups have the same sort of power over their followers as a gnostic cult like the Manichaeans had in the fourth century. At their heart is a chamber of secrets to which only a few have access. Because human beings are innately curious and passionately ambitious to know what only a few have ever known, the secret of the universe, those on the outside are zealous and disciplined to prove their worth to the powers-that-be at the center.

Why is gnosticism so important for Johnson in the story of modern times? In this book and in others (especially the one called *Intellectuals*) it's clear that Johnson, like Burke, believes that intellectuals insert "a great danger into political thought." In previous ages, intellectuals were only advisors at the seat of power. If they were lucky, they worked there for the nobility and other propertied men; otherwise, they played a marginal role clerking and teaching for small pay. All that changed in the age of politics. Modern times is the invention of intellectuals, and now they are running the government. It's assumed that the complexity of society requires the special sight of "knowers," experts in highly specialized subjects. By identifying the gnosticism present in modern times, Johnson is diagnosing the problem of modern times through a study of Christianity and of writers like Burke.

The French experiment, Burke predicted, was inherently unstable, and that has proved to be the case. Since Burke's time two empires and four republics have come and gone in France. Political philosophers like Rousseau and Paine began with individual freedom as the supreme good, but they ended with the State as the supreme power. Here's the opening for instability, and here's the opening for intellectuals. Until the state naturally withers away, it can't be just an abstraction. It has to exist. It has to be run by people, and it's best run by those "knowers" who can manage the hidden structures intellectuals themselves have uncovered. Only they can rise above the inherent contradictions. Gnostics are the philosophers, the economists, the anthropologists, the sociologists, and experts in a whole host of other disciplines who have mastered these patterns. They are the vanguard that can usher in the peace and tranquility of the socialist paradise. Paul Johnson has written *Modern Times* to debunk this self-image of gnostics. Many may mean well, but in practice they are the main character in the tragedy of modern times.

Object Lessons

The theme of choice is central to this study of the force that binds a country together. To do justice to the theme, it's important to emphasize the difference between the embeddedness of the individual that's such an essential part of Burke's political philosophy and the determinism that characterizes Marxism and structuralism. They both de-emphasize individual choice, but they strongly differ in the locus of power. In Burke, the individual consents to meeting obligations "not chosen but binding"; his participation is "a kind of choice." In Marxism and structuralism the individual has no agency. The course of history is determined by forces beyond an individual's control. Those gnostics who have been admitted into the chamber of secrets are the only ones with authority to interpret what the forces require of the rest of us. And if an individual doesn't agree and insists on the freedom of his will, he is judged to be a mental defective, as Freud claimed in his own battles with heresy, or he is compelled to submit. This drama is now playing on campuses all across the country.

I decided to write about this difference when I read the following sentence from Johnson's opening chapter. In it he elaborates on Marx's theory that the "inner but concealed essential pattern" of things is very different from the way things appear to look:

> *On the surface, men appeared to be exercising their free will, taking decisions, determining events. In reality, to those familiar with the methods of dialectical materialism, such individuals, however powerful, were seen to be mere flotsam, hurled hither and thither by the irresistible surges of economic forces.*

I read the passage soon after finishing the essays on Burke. It struck me with some force that it was much like what I had just written about Chaucer's Palamon and Arcite in the first of the essays on *The Great Debate*. To recap briefly, the two knights almost simultaneously catch a glimpse of a beautiful woman wandering in the garden below their prison cell, and they subsequently devote the rest of their lives to possessing her for themselves. They, too, seem to be exercising their free will as individuals. They make many decisions in furtherance of their goal, but, while nominally free, they remain slaves to their attachment.

For Chaucer, Shakespeare, and comedy in general, though, a character who drunkenly drifts through life obsessing over the image of a beautiful object (which can be a political objective) will carry on like this only in the first half of the story. The situation will have to change because a person with an obsessive attachment is bound for a crack-up. Just as they say that nature abhors a vacuum, nature abhors a fixed idea. Comedy maintains that, under the right conditions, Everyman is capable of waking from the enchantment of an idea or image that drives him crazy; the object can then take its place in a larger intelligence. Once the mistake is cleared up, Everyman may discover that the situation is quite agreeable, even wonderful. This contact with a larger intelligence, even if it's only for a moment, is wisdom, a brief touch or a glimpse of that which "the Lord formed from the beginning before he created anything else."

As part of my argument, I fancy a structuralist ripe for comedy. It doesn't occur to him that the thing driving him crazy about the way things are might be a misunderstanding or a misperception of his own. Instead, he watches characters running around like chickens with their heads cut off and is satisfied with it as a representation of other human beings and of behavior determined by a social structure. Magically immune to the craziness, he's inspired to fix it by fundamentally changing the structure. Thus begins a career that, for those in the audience, looks like lunacy; the poor man hasn't factored his own craziness into it. We watch as he builds a system that's the architectural equivalent of painting himself into a corner. Escher's "Relativity" gives us a picture of it. If there's no up or down, there's no stairway to a comic ending. The structuralist may have set out to build a better mousetrap, but he trapped himself and everyone else in the maze instead.

A comedy depends for its effect on characters who consent to a comic ending. If you believe that individuals in a story are not really individuals and a narrative about them is just a bourgeois construct, so much for life, liberty, and the pursuit of happiness. If structuralists believe that human beings are wholly determined by the culture and there's no waking from it, then how are they able to critique the culture as if they were objective, independent observers and actors? Or are knowers like themselves—the members of an elect devoted to an esoteric theory—the only ones who can be awakened?

Great comedy is as direct and simple as a pedestrian absorbed in reading his Blackberry slipping on a banana peel. A character who claims a superior intelligence for peering into hidden patterns serves as the object lesson. The poor man has fallen in love with his own intelligence, and this has the worst kind of narrowing effect. Comedy arranges things so we can heartily laugh at those who pretend to speak with a divine authority. There may be no tonic better than watching a good production of Tartuffe for those who suffer from the disorder (or for those who suffer from people who suffer from the disorder). Gnostics guard their elixirs as the exclusive property of a special intelligence or a specially educated class of people. Just as their disorder is common, though, the tonic is free to everyone. Because a comic vision contains the experiences of countless generations, it expresses that which is as germane for the continuation of human life as any ever devised.

The Standard That Was Never Lost

Admittedly, Burke's emphasis on obligations is a hard sell. In popular culture choice is a kind of fetish, but comedy continues to be a popular form of entertainment. In comedy the free will of a character in love with his own idea turns out to be a parody of freedom. The character's safety and health, his freedom, actually depend on whether the mind can open to a larger intelligence, and the opening depends on something—like a banana peel under the foot of an unwary pedestrian—that can upend him, turn him upside down, and empty his ideas out like loose change in his pocket. Can the pedestrian take credit for that? Can he call his fall a choice? People of all stripes have these experiences, maybe not every day but often enough. Again and again we have them until they form a sort of pattern, a meaningful string of cautionary tales. Recognizing the pattern is a saving grace.

When I'm right in the middle of doing something important, my golden retriever regularly barks at the door. Do I have a choice whether to take her for a walk or not? I do, sort of. But I have learned from experience since she was a puppy that not walking her is going to be an even larger disruption in my life. Also, from my own experience I wouldn't want a natural bodily urge subject to the whim of a gate-keeper. Do I feel obligated to take her out? Not if I factor in why we have her in our lives in the first place. She and our Cavalier King Charles Spaniel are an endless source of comic relief and comfort. They are rescue dogs in that they have rescued us from petty thoughts and moods time and time again. We treasure them the way one treasures good health and sanity. Rather than an obligation, taking her out is an expression of her embeddedness in our lives and our embeddedness in hers. So to return to the language I found in Yuval Levin's book on Burke, the decision to stop what I'm doing and take her out "is a kind of choice." I have chosen a way of life which includes her, and the barking and walking are a part of that. This recognition is a small matter, and yet it and the thousands of similar recognitions which make up the fabric of our lives add up and point to a coherent something, a force which is greater than a self-interest narrowly defined, a purpose which is sensible and which moves us to do what needs to be done. Whether you call it wisdom, a transcendent standard of government, or free will it stands for something, for a vision that marries obligation and freedom. This "something" is the standard that was never lost, despite those who insist we have been inevitably and forever inaugurated into an age of moral relativism.

Modern Times, as I wrote earlier, is a dismal story. It surveys what Johnson calls the Age of Politics. My wife and I have been to ground zero of this age, the camps built up around the railroad hub of Auschwitz in Poland. Himmler decided to build the camp there for a reason, and the camps came into existence for a reason. They are the dead end hub of politics as defined by a man like that. When we were there, we said prayers for the lives lost and made our way out of that place. We leave it there, but it still exists, a massive black hole. Let us pray, then, that it has drawn into itself the deadly nightshade of that time.

It's still there down that black hole, though, and some would bring it back. So I say, as Burke did, that whether we do or not "is a kind of choice." Why not choose to let the poison lie where it lies, and ring in instead an Age of Comedy with glasses full of fellowship and side splitting laughter. Let's have "Comedy Tonight!" and return to basics, to that which is rooted in human nature and our culture, but which can only exist if it's fresh and full of life like the deep well-springs and warmth of comedy.

Chapter Nine:
The Only Kind of
Freedom That Matters

Fra Angelico's *The Conversion of St. Augustine*

Introduction

I studied *A History of Christianity* by Paul Johnson over the last few months of 2015 and completed this essay just before Christmas. The shorter days were marked as well with the lives cut short by the attacks in San Bernardino and Paris.

Since gnosticism played such an important role in *Modern Times*, I wanted in particular to learn what Johnson had to say about it in his history of Christianity, but the question about gnosticism gradually took its place within the larger narrative as to why Christianity managed to survive at all. This essay is about the first chapter called "The Rise and Rescue of the Jesus Sect." I realized near the end of its composition that for all intents and purposes it was a Christmas message, perhaps because Johnson wrote his history in that spirit, so I sent it to my three siblings. We no longer live in the same house together, but the spirit of Christmas, I believe, still abides in us. For children who grew up loving it as the day of all days, how could it not.

The Rise of the Jesus Sect

The universality of the message preached first by Jesus and then by Paul is the most important theme of the chapter. The Roman Empire, Johnson points out, played an important role in the success of that message. The Pax Romana opened up a vast area made up of diverse cultures to the free movement of people, goods, and services. By concentrating the responsibilities for government in Rome, the empire also relieved people of their civic duties to the polis, the immediate city where they lived. Because the Roman state religion made no demands on private belief and didn't "touch the heart," a person "thus had time, opportunity, and above all motive to develop his private sphere and explore his own individual and personal responsibilities." People could concern themselves with questions like "Who am I? Where am I going? What do I believe?"

There were hundreds of gods and cults that flourished throughout the empire, many of them imports from the East, but these were mainly concerned with ethics and said nothing "about the soul and its future, and its relationship to the universe and eternity." It was a world, writes Johnson, ready for God. Within the relative security of the Pax Romana, a religious message—which had its origins in a small Eastern province but which transcended parochial, tribal concerns—could travel in all directions to resonate with people far beyond its borders.

The Jews had God, but He but was closely tied to His people and their promised land. In Johnson's opinion, Jesus understood that it would have to reformed in order to become a universal religion and that this was a primary goal of his ministry. Also, Judaism during the time of Jesus was divided between Samaritans, Essenes, Sadducees, and Pharisees. Collectively, they were weakened because they fought among themselves, and so the Romans occupied the country with force and ruled them. The Roman occupation, while welcomed by some collaborators, was a national embarrassment.

It's an essential characteristic of Judaism that, especially from the time of the Exodus, Jews saw history as a reflection of God's activity. They had "imagination to relate history to speculation," a blending of the real and the ideal "which is the religious dynamic." Many Jews at the time of Jesus, therefore, saw the troubles in their land as a judgment on their obedience to God's laws. They believed, based on scripture, that a Messiah would come to drive out the oppressors in an apocalyptic battle and that subsequently "God alone would rule in Israel." This was the message of John the Baptist. Before the apocalypse, he taught, people should repent their sins and be baptized. John's message was very simple, and he's the link between the reformist movements in Judaism and Jesus.

About forty years after the death of Jesus, the Jews of Israel did fight an apocalyptic battle to drive the Romans out of their land, but they lost. The Jews were driven out instead, and Jerusalem was leveled. When viewed from the perspective of history, the death of Jerusalem mirrors the death on the cross of Jesus. The Romans thought they could extinguish the problems posed by Jesus by killing him, and forty years later they thought they could neutralize the whole Jewish question by leveling their city.

A historian, however, enjoys a larger view of these events. It's a comic vision because it reveals the smallness of people's ideas when compared to greatness of things-as-they-are in a much larger time and space. The opening chapters of Johnson's history tells the story of how the God of Judaism eventually conquered the Roman Empire in the form of Christianity. It's a story which witnesses to the power of the message initiated by an obscure teacher in a far away corner of the empire. Then, too, we know that Judaism survived as well in diaspora communities, but this is a story Johnson reserves for *A History of the Jews*.

The Donation of Life and the Obligations of Love

Having studied Johnson's history of Christianity and other books by him, I'm convinced he views history as a reflection of God's activity. It's why his books find a place in these essays about the existence of a moral order. Johnson approaches the subject with great seriousness and purpose. As he tells the story of Christianity, it's clear that some of the characters in it are heroes, some are villains, and others, like Constantine and some early doctors of the church, are a complex mixture. Apart from Jesus himself, Paul of Tarsus is the greatest hero in Johnson's rendering of the story. Without Paul there would be no Christianity. From the moment he encountered the risen Jesus, Paul understood the universality of Jesus' message, and he worked tirelessly to make it known to the ends of the Roman empire. Near the end of his evangelizing, he made it known in Rome itself, for his most important letter is addressed to Romans.

There's a passage in *A History of Christianity* that explains why Paul matters so much to Paul Johnson:

> Paul is an obstacle to those who wish to turn Christianity into a closed
> system. He believed in freedom. For him Christianity was the only kind
> of freedom that matters, the liberation from the law, and the donation

of life. He associated freedom with truth, for which he had an unlimited reverence. And in pursuing truth he established the right to think, and to think through to the ultimate conclusion. The process of inquiry, in fact, mirrored his salvation theology: he accepted the obligations of love, but not the authority of scholarship and tradition. He established the right to think in the full Hellenistic sense and thus showed that the Christian faith has nothing to fear from the power of thought.

A history is a reflection of God's activity only when it's joined with the pursuit of truth that Johnson finds in Paul's ministry. This sets a high standard. When I read Paul Johnson, though, from the density, depth, and scope of his research (his knowledge of literature, philosophy, and economics as well as history) and from the great coherence and consistency with which he develops the major themes of his large undertakings, I sense the passion for truth he so admires in Paul.

That passion is reflected in the quality as well as the quantity of his writing. For example, the statement that Paul "accepted the obligations of love, but not the authority of scholarship and tradition" condenses the dynamic within Paul that will animate many pages of the history that follows in his wake. Love, for him, was the only law that mattered. For a Pharisee like Paul—that is, a lawyer specifically trained to explain and enforce the law—this is a revolutionary turnabout. But Johnson makes it clear that the love he's talking about is not just a warm and fuzzy sentiment or the prompting of desire. It's a discipline which involves the whole man, heart and mind, in the deepest inquiry of which it is capable. It's a love for and an obligation to the truth.

Paul, like the Greek culture all around him when he was growing up in cosmopolitan Tarsus, is concerned with how we know the world, and his answer is a blending of East and West—the philosophers of Greece who know the world through a passionate relationship with Ideas and the prophets of Judaism who know the world through a passionate relationship with the God of Israel. When Johnson writes that Paul accepted the obligations of love, he's framing the issue as to what governs human beings in this world. Is it love for an idea, our names for things, or for something else, something beyond thought? Paul was a visionary, but his letters give us a palpable sense of him as a writer wrestling with words and thoughts to express the truth of his vision.

Johnson writes of Jesus that his teaching is "more a series of glimpses, or matrices, a collection of insights, rather than a code of doctrine." Jesus is not a simple figure. He taught something that was "hard to grasp." Our glimpses of him from the different accounts "invites comment, interpretation, elaboration and constructive argument, and is the starting point for rival, though compatible, lines of inquiry." For Johnson the variety and confusion about him from the different texts "is essentially part of Jesus's universalist posture: the wonder is that the personality behind the mission is in no way fragmented but is always integrated and true to character. Jesus contrives to be all things to all men while remaining faithful to himself." This last observation may explain why there is such thematic consistency in texts that stretch from Paul in the first century to Shakespeare in the sixteenth. Jesus' donation of his own life continues to command our attention.

For Paul there's a link between that donation and the gift of life to himself and to all who live, and writers like Chaucer and Shakespeare continue to wonder at it. For Chaucer and for Shakespeare God is love, and in all their works they help us to understand the implications of that. Since both "The Knight's Tale" and *A Midsummer Night's Dream* take place in pagan times, the love that's their subject is not the divine love of a crucified savior. By removing the Christian context, they aim to show that the love of an ordinary person has a special power. It exists in us all, but it has to be exposed to a refining fire before we can appreciate its true value.

The love that preserves us and others comes to life when it dawns on us the importance of what we have been given. The salvation theology (or mechanism, as Johnson sometimes calls it) in Paul's Christianity refers to a deep understanding of the obligation Jesus fulfilled by donating his life the way he did. In Chaucer's and Shakespeare's renderings of this story (which are essentially comedies) the mechanism is a wake-up call, the sudden puncturing of an idea on which a person thought his entire existence depended. Even the briefest glimpse of not-being (as he's accustomed to be) forces a person to consider the nature of being in its true light. Seeing in this way (with the eyes, Shakespeare writes) is a miracle, like the birth of a child (even ourselves) into the world. Everyone can experience these moments of insight, appreciation, and gratitude. It's not just for rocket scientists or theologians. Through compact phrases, "the donation of life" and "the obligations of love" Johnson gives us Christianity as Paul understood it.

The Death of God and a Seed of Freedom

There's something indestructible in the story, even though it involves a death, the death of God in fact; and the death of God, of course, concerns us in our own time, even if we're not aware of the issue as such. There's plenty of evidence, trumpeted by thousands of pundits, that people in the West are trending away from Christianity and have been for centuries now. Nevertheless, it still carries the seed of freedom that Paul found in his vision on the road to Damascus, quite unaffected by the opinion of pundits. We learn from Augustine's Confessions that at a critical time of his life in the garden at Milan, he heard the voice of a child tell him, "Tolle. Lege." Take up. Read. When he did take up his book and read, he found there release from the weight of his old life. For Johnson, Christianity is still a book ready to be opened and read. For those of us whose tastes run to secular texts, we have Johnson's own book to take up and read.

The donation of life, so lovingly depicted in the Christian story by the birth of Jesus, perennially comes round to us as the days grow shorter. This year it has come upon us in a darkening time of past and impending violence from a death cult which would put a sudden and final end to the freedom and even the life we enjoy. Johnson's history reminds us that, when we inquire into the truth of it, Christianity still shows signs of life. Like a good physician, though, we have to examine it carefully to find the source of its distempers and take steps to allow its natural vitality to reassert itself.

What exactly is the discipline, the medicine, that will restore that natural vitality? Who, with some authority in the business, can tell us? Johnson himself is a Catholic, but he knows too much about the Church's history to take his marching orders from the Vatican. After reading his book, I'm persuaded that, along with the stability of an established Church, he values the freedom of conscience that's the hallmark of Protestantism. It's a freedom that Pope John XXIII—who was a historian like Johnson, not a theologian like the previous pope—advocated (up to a point) in the reforms of Vatican II.

Paul Johnson's reading of Christianity reminds us that we are free to look into these questions for ourselves with help from the most reliable guides we can find. Nevertheless, for those who haven't carefully studied them, the letters of Paul, I think he would say, are a good place to start.

Chapter Ten:

Does Not Wisdom Call Out?

William Blake's *Ancient of Days*

Part One: The Matrices

Introduction

A. Paul: The First Rescue

This essay on *A History of Christianity* is structured around Paul Johnson's judgment that the teaching of Jesus is "more a series of glimpses, or matrices, a collection of insights, rather than a code of doctrine." Johnson is a great historian and a great writer, but his books are not easy to read. The content of a chapter moves from paragraph to paragraph without a break over a wide range of topics for give or take sixty pages. Because the reader must find and thoroughly consider the matrices around which his purpose gathers, Johnson challenges his readers, perhaps the way Jesus did, to figure things out for themselves based on the structure he has built into the whole. This reading, therefore, seeks out those insights in the uninterrupted flow of the narrative. While faithful to Johnson's text, I also have added commentaries and examples drawn from my own reading and experiences.

The first chapter, "The Rise and Rescue of the Jesus Sect," begins with the ministries of Jesus and Paul and then takes us through the history of the Church for the next two hundred years, including the contributions of Tertullian, Origen, and Cyprian of Carthage. The Jesus Sect, of course, rises with Jesus himself, but the movement very quickly fell apart when their leader was killed. When the movement did regroup after the resurrection, the appearances, and Pentecost, the Jerusalem Church remained closely allied to Temple worship and the Judaic law; it was in the process, Johnson writes, of being absorbed back into Judaism. In Johnson's opinion, Paul's vision of the risen Christ and his mission to the gentiles preserved the true teaching—that is, the universality of it. The two movements collided when Paul met with the pillars of the Jerusalem

Church in AD 49. From Paul's own account of it, he left that meeting convinced that he had a divine mandate to take his message to the gentiles. When the Romans leveled the city of Jerusalem twenty years later, the Jerusalem Church ceased to exist, and Paul's epistles and his congregations became the most important vehicles for the new faith. His interpretation of Jesus' message and his efforts to communicate it throughout the empire are the first rescue of the Jesus Sect.

B. The Need for Another Rescue

Johnson maintains that, contrary to histories by early church writers, there was no established Church for about 150 years. There was the Pauline gospel which "stood a good chance of surviving and spreading. But it had no organization behind it. Paul did not believe in such a thing. He believed in the Spirit, working through him and others. Why should a man regulate when the Spirit would do it for him? And of course he did not want a fixed system with rules and laws." Jesus, Paul believed, had come to earth to deliver believers from the law. This was what he understood from his encounter with the risen Christ.

Thanks to modern research, we know more about the early history of the church than Eusebius, its first important historian, did in the fourth century. Eusebius had his own reasons to make claims for an Apostolic Age and a primitive church established by Jesus himself. The claims, though, are not supported by the evidence. Instead of a seamless transition from Jesus to the twelve and their churches, there were a multitude of Christian cults "swarming to survive" in the first and second centuries. In later centuries these groups saw the advantage of tracing their ancestry back to an apostle in order to legitimize their bishop and his see, but many of these "succession lists" were fictions. Johnson compares the survival of these groups to a Darwinian process of natural selection. Christianity once again would have to be rescued, this time from dissolving into separate cults swarming to survive.

The Tension Between Two Forms of Regulation

A. The Law and the Spirit

Johnson points out that the cults had two distinctive shapes. From AD 50 to 200, he writes, they were either Christian gnostics, rationalists who prided themselves on their knowledge of a sacred code of truth, or revivalists gathered around charismatics, ecstatic worshippers who believed in the Spirit as opposed to a fixed system of rules and laws. The difference between these two introduces an important tension in the history of Christianity that existed from the beginning. The quote at the beginning of the essay notes the matrices, as opposed to doctrines, in the teaching of Jesus, and Johnson then goes on to write in that passage that the teaching "is a starting point for rival, though compatible, lines of inquiry...It inaugurates a religion of dialogue, exploration, and experiment. Its radical elements are balanced by conservative qualifications, there is a constant mixture of legalism and antinomianism [a worship that rejects the Law in favor of the Spirit], and the emphasis repeatedly switches from rigor and militancy [justified by legalism] to acquiescence and the acceptance of suffering." The tension between the two informs a great deal of the material in Johnson's history. More importantly, the tension between them forms something like an electric field of positive and negative energies.

The matrix was present in Judaism as well. For example, the sacrifice of Isaac dramatizes the most fundamental tension imaginable between obedience to the word of God and the deepest obligation of the spirit that moves an individual human being. It's a story that blows up for all time our ideas about the law, obedience, or the obligations of love, and it conveys an overwhelming imperative: the world and the demands of an ethical life will always be larger than our conceptions of them even if those conceptions come from God himself. This ultimate test of obedience exists in tension with the gift of a good life, for God blessed Abraham with the freedom of his spirit when He called him out of Haram, promised him the land, and undertook to multiply his offspring. These encounters have meaning not only for him but for everyone, for He adds, "And in thy seed shall all the nations of the earth be blessed." The promises of land and human flourishing are the essential fruits of Abraham's election; the law comes later.

B. Two Capitals: Athens and Jerusalem

The preceding section describes a matrix that is extremely important to the story Paul Johnson would tell, but the currents of it are capable of producing significant eddies around which other insights can gather. For early Christians the law, a rationalization of human behavior and belief, had two capitals. If you were a cosmopolitan Greek or Roman, it was Athens. If you were evangelized by Christian Zealots and Essenes in Africa, it was Jerusalem. Tertullian, the second century bishop and theologian from Carthage, asked rhetorically "What does Athens have to do with Jerusalem?" implying that it has nothing to do with it. Nevertheless, Tertullian had to address the issue because for many centuries there had been a tension between the two in Judaism as well as the early church. For example, when the Seleucid king Antiochus Epiphanes ruled Jerusalem, the Maccabees revolted to reduce the power of Hellenism and Hellenizing Judaism. Because Greeks had such an influence, the Jews of the time lived within a matrix or a gravitational field created by the positive and negative powers of the two cultures.

It might help to picture the field between Athens and Jerusalem in an example closer to our own time. Diaspora Jews who had been assimilated into modern states all over Europe and America during the 19th and early 20th centuries lived in it. Despite the enormous power that Jewish Orthodoxy had in their families and communities, many were attracted by the rational, empirical knowledge of the West that owes so much to the world view of the Greeks. I came to appreciate this tension more fully through the stories and novels of Isaac Bashevis Singer who recreates for us what it was like for Eastern European Jews to live under the influence of two very different worlds—that of their host country and that of their ancient faith.

Tertullian posed his question about Athens and Jerusalem to warn Christians away from reasoning about something that couldn't be reasoned about. He believed, Tertullian wrote, "because it was absurd." His question also describes the tension that had such an effect on Jews like Singer who grew up in Poland between the wars. For Jews who survived, the Second World War ended the uneasy accommodations they had achieved in the ghetto. In later fiction Singer tells the story of those who had been taught by their faith to love God but who found it impossible to do so after the Holocaust. These portraits of human hearts in postwar Europe and America match the power of their models in the Biblical narratives.

What *does* empiricism and enlightenment have to do with the law when countries like Germany and Italy, so integral to the cultural history of Europe, can fall so far into barbarism? The history of the West, I believe, achieved a kind of end time during the 20th Century, and camps like Auschwitz are ground zero of that history. Since these essays are an inquiry into the existence of a moral order and since this is the most important question for people living in modern times, it follows for me that Singer is the most compelling writer of fiction in the 20th Century. (Isaac's sacrifice, the Maccabees' revolt, and the material about Eastern European Jews are my examples, not Johnson's.)

C. The Founders: The Creative Power Within the Field

The stories about Jesus in the gospels also reveal that he lived and taught in a gravitational field between the power of the Law in scripture and the power of his Spirit as he spoke to the people and healed them. Jesus, writes Johnson, "was a practicing Jew from a conformist background, learned in the faith, and with a deep respect for Jewish tradition." But Johnson also emphasizes that "the core of his teaching couldn't be contained within a Jewish framework" for the following reasons: he had a new interpretation of God; he claimed divine status as God's messenger; he taught a new mechanism of salvation; and he taught that a man could be justified without the law. When he was tested about his knowledge of the law and answered in a capital case, "Let he who is without fault cast the first stone," he conveys the common sense of a man who has lived in the world as well as a divine loving kindness. A sentence like that is part of a story, not a law, and yet it conveys timeless wisdom with the power of scripture. It's an expression of the Spirit that moved him to speak and to heal. (This example is mine, not Johnson's.)

We gather from his letters that Paul lived and taught in the field between the polarities of Athens and Jerusalem about which Tertullian complained. Judaism in Paul's day was centered on Temple worship in Jerusalem and the rules laid out in the Bible for the sacrifices there and for daily living. Paul grew up in Tarsus, however, a long way from Jerusalem, where he was exposed to Greek philosophy and traditions of inquiry. The city was known as the Athens of Asia Minor. Perhaps as a kind of armor against Hellenization and Hellenizing Judaism, Paul began his adult life as a Pharisee militantly enforcing the law, but on the road to Damascus he experienced "a sea change into something rich and strange." (Shakespeare, I believe, is deeply indebted to the writings of Paul.) Like a man set free from gravity underwater, he now was guided by the Spirit of the risen Christ. Just as an electric generator cuts through polarities of positive and negative, Paul's vision of the life, death, and resurrection of Jesus conveys power, not logical or legal certainty. Nevertheless, like the Greek philosophers, he sought the truth and transformed the truth of his vision—in which the land promised to Abraham has been changed into the richness and strangeness of the Kingdom—into words and sentences that would appeal to Greek and Latin gentiles.

Paul's most important epistle informs the Romans that in his gospel "the righteousness of God is revealed." Since it's the "righteousness" of God that's revealed, Paul is teaching them about the God of Abraham, Isaac, and Jacob for whom the only freedom that matters is a life lived in obedience to Him. But for the next eleven chapters Paul reasons with his readers as to the nature of that righteousness and how a person is justified by it. Again and again he engages the issue, moving it forward a little each time, and then looking at it from its new position. According to Johnson, Romans is the most important inquiry into the truth of these matters in the New Testament. Paul is a writer who, with the greatest urgency and with heartfelt reasons, appealed to the hearts and minds of those who would live a life commensurate with God's gift of life. (I have added the quote from Romans to introduce Johnson's commentary on the epistle.)

D. Gnostics and Charismatics at Opposite Ends of the Matrix

Johnson writes of Jesus that he is not "a simple figure. His actions and motives were complex and he taught something which was hard to grasp." He goes on to add, however, that "the wonder is that the personality behind the mission is in no way fragmented but is always integrated and true to character. Jesus contrives to be all things to all men while remaining faithful to himself." The phrase "all things to all men" comes from Paul's description of himself and his ministry in 1 Corinthians so we can infer that he, too, saw the generation of power in his ministry as a kind of balancing act. From reading Johnson's history we can also infer that the leaders of the church who came after them weren't as integrated or as successful at finding the balance.

Of course, they can't possibly imitate Christ, much as they might try. Marcion, a brilliant convert from the Greek colony of Pontus on the Black Sea, was a follower of Paul who lived about 60 years after Paul's martyrdom. Like Paul, he sought that which was true, but he pursued this goal by studying the many texts attributed to Paul in order to determine which epistles were actually written by the apostle and which were not. He was a scholar, and his focus was on the word, rather than the flesh, of Jesus. He had, as Johnson describes it, "a plain unspectacular philosophy of love," and this description of it contrasts sharply with Paul's vision of the risen Christ. Marcion accepted only seven of Paul's letters as authentic, and he rejected the Old Testament entirely for it seemed, Johnson writes, "to be talking of a quite different God: monstrous, evil-creating, bloody, the patron of ruffians like David." In the tradition of Greek philosophy Marcion rationalized the New Testament canon by rooting out inauthentic texts and by breaking with its roots in Judaism. This is the path of gnosticism—the focus on a text or a code, the rejection of the flesh including the flesh of Jesus, and the rejection of the Old Testament God and his Creation. Gnosticism represents the triumph of the Idea and a return to Plato, an interpretation that would appeal to Greek and Roman intellectuals.

Charismatics gather around the other pole of the matrix. Paul's conception of the church as "a community where the spirit worked through individuals, rather than an organized hierarchy" encouraged those who would be a "free-lance, self-appointed proclaimer of truth." For example, Montanus, who called himself the Paraclete (which in Christianity refers to the Holy Spirit), led a very successful charismatic movement in Rome. Orthodox Christians were especially concerned with how Montanus inspired many women to join his movement. Because he allowed them to teach, Tertullian attacked him as a heretic. For Johnson, Tertullian offers "a unique glimpse into the workings of the early church." This refers, I believe, to the way Tertullian was attracted both to the rules of orthodoxy and to the truth of the Spirit. Because of the Montanists' "impeccable rectitude and burning faith" in the Spirit, late in life Tertullian rejected his earlier judgment and joined their movement.

Having presented these portraits of men who lived in the early days of the church, Johnson sums up the tension between the polarities of the matrix in the following sentence:

> Just as the varieties of gnosticism risked capturing the Church's personality and absorbing it into a disintegrating mess of sub-Hellenic cults, so the charismatics might submerge the Church's unitary voice under a Babel of "prophecies."

There was danger on both extremes. The rationalists risked losing the universality of the Christian message by insisting on a very narrow, purified version of it. On the other side of the spectrum, charlatans took advantage of people's emotions and corrupted the universality of message with a Babel of voices. Despite the threat from both extremes, Johnson argues through the rest of the chapter that the field between them would shape the church into a coherent vessel for weathering the storms of time and circumstance.

Two Basic Types of Christians

Johnson contrasts Marcion and Tertullian in order to mark another eddy in the matrix. Just as there are two kinds of law within the matrix, these 2nd Century figures, he tells us, represent "two basic types of Christians: the rational optimist who believes that the love-principle is sufficient, man having an essential desire to do good, and the pessimist, convinced of the essential corruptibility of human creatures and the need for the mechanism of damnation." Both positions can claim they are derived from Paul's teaching. Marcion, the rationalist scholar, "stripped the New Testament down to its bare Pauline bones" in order to focus on the optimistic promises of Paul's authentic teaching. In keeping with this optimism, Marcion rejected the notion that God would use fear as a force "to compel obedience." Tertullian, who believed "because it is absurd," disparaged intellectual inquiry, a powerful form of persuasion in Paul's letters. Tertullian thought it was foolishness to merely forbid sin; without fear human beings would stray easily into temptation. Rather than a cosmopolitan, worldly reasonableness, he embodied a militant form of Christianity. For him, Johnson writes, "The Church was a precious elite of believers to be defended against contamination from whatever quarter; the Devil, he thought, roamed the earth seeking to corrupt." Nevertheless, Johnson argues that Tertullian "sprang from the Pauline tradition. He stressed the overwhelming power of faith, the precious gift of the elect. To him, Christians were supermen because the spirit moved in them."

The Christian matrix which contains these two basic types is remarkably similar to Thomas Sowell's depiction of the two predominant visions in modern American politics. I have written before in these essays about the importance of *A Conflict of Visions: Ideological Origins of Political Struggles* for *A Comic Vision of Great Constancy* and for these essays. Sowell's second chapter, "Constrained and Unconstrained Visions," begins with the crux of his entire argument. He writes, "Social visions differ in their basic conceptions of the nature of man," and he devotes the rest of the chapter to contrasting the constrained and the unconstrained points of view.

Sowell relies on the writings of William Godwin and the Marquis de Condorcet to present the unconstrained vision. Because Godwin lived at the end of the 18th Century, he reflects the optimism of Enlightenment philosophies. Intellectuals during that time were convinced that philosophers like Newton had revealed the laws of nature and that these laws were truer and more useful than Christian superstitions. They assumed that, just as human beings could calculate the forces of gravity, human beings could calculate the best way to regulate other human beings. The success of the scientific method in harnessing the forces of nature encouraged them to believe that egocentric behavior was not a feature of human nature but of poorly constructed societies. Godwin writes, "Men are capable no doubt, of preferring an inferior interest of their own to a superior interest of others; but this preference arises from a combination of circumstances and is not the necessary and invariable law of nature." Given the right circumstances (which political philosophers like Godwin will create for them), human beings have the "essential desire to do good."

To present the constrained view, Sowell relies on the writings of Adam Smith, Edmund Burke, and Friedrich Hayek. They construct their ethical and political theories on a pessimistic vision of human nature which undoubtedly derives from the deeply rooted Christian view (made canonical in the writings of Augustine) that there's an unbridgeable gap between the powers of God and man. Their 18th Century secular version of it drops the devil's prominent role, as in Tertullian's version of human nature and its temptations, to emphasize human ignorance rather than human sinfulness. They accept "the basic constraint" that human beings can't possibly know everything. Consequently, our decisions are morally constrained. This basic constraint is increased by the fact that human beings are inherently self-interested. Despite their pessimism about human nature, however, these writers are optimistic about the existence of a moral order, as I have shown in these essays. Smith's optimism is reflected in the impartial spectator that regulates our desire to be loved and to be lovable. Burke's optimism is reflected in a transcendent standard for government which emerges as human beings discover, through a process of natural selection, those social customs and institutions that allow their societies to survive and prosper.

The Matrices and Johnson's Critique of Modern Intellectuals

That Johnson and Sowell have arrived at such a similar matrix from different angles of vision speaks to something constant either in human nature or in the West's interpretation of it. In the passage quoted earlier in the essay Johnson identifies "a constant mixture of legalism and antinomianism" in the life and message of Jesus. While the tension between these two forms of "regulation" leads to some bewilderment and confusion on the part of his disciples, for Johnson the mixture is "essentially part of Jesus's universalist posture." To fully represent this posture, the spirit and the law must be hitched together—like the love and marriage of two strong, autonomous partners. Like any relationship, though, there's going to be some strain and confusion between the two. From Johnson's history of Christianity we learn that the path to a partnership between them is as bewildering as the courtships in *A Midsummer Night's Dream*. The lovers' stories, which picture relationships at different stages of a person's life (including the timelessness of immortals), dramatize for us that a strong partnership is and is always going to involve a bewildering mixture of constraint and freedom, freedom and constraint. The confusion is part and parcel of human nature, for the nature of love itself involves a tension between freedom and constraint. Even more confusing, it can be a bewildering mixture of love and hate.

The similarity between the matrix present in early Christianity and in modern political structures is, I believe, of great interest to Paul Johnson. The tension between the law and the spirit creates an intellectual field that functions like a system of checks and balances. An emphasis on the Spirit checked and reformed the legalism policed by the Pharisees. But even in his lifetime Paul checked charismatics like those Corinthians who claimed that, once possessed by the spirit, they were above the law and could break with impunity common sense rules of behavior. Paul warned them that their pride, the great temptation to become "puffed up," was completely contrary to the true spirit of the risen Christ.

I read *Intellectuals*—Johnson's book about the rise of public intellectuals since the 18th Century Age of Enlightenment—before reading his history of Christianity. I'm now convinced that Johnson finds a strong similarity between the gnostics who pride themselves on the purity of their rationalizations, the puffed up charismatics who believe they are above the law because they have been possessed by the spirit, and the modern intellectuals he catalogues in his book named after them. Modern intellectuals, who run the gamut from logicians like Bertrand Russell to Romantic poets like Shelly, make their mark in the public arena either as rationalists or as charismatics, but they haven't successfully integrated the forces within the matrices outlined by the teachings of Jesus. Paul Johnson's rebuke of them was inspired, I imagine, by the character of Jesus himself, the spirit of Paul's epistles, and Johnson's study of the church's history.

Part Two: A Mighty Fortress

The Gradual Emergence of Orthodoxy

A. Bishops and the Writings

The rest of the first chapter documents what happened when Paul's idea of the church, "the spirit working through individuals, not a hierarchy," could not maintain the Jesus Sect as a coherent movement. After the Jerusalem Church ceased to exist, the movement found shelter around two institutional pillars that gradually assumed an apostolic authority: the bishops who led churches in major cities and an orthodox New Testament. The free lancing of late second century charismatics like Montanus and the threat from Christian gnostic sects gave these pillars a reason for being. Johnson's explanation for their rise is much like Yuval Levin's explanation for the rise of Burke's transcendent standard of government as English society evolved. The function of a bishop and the final shape of the canon came into being by a process of natural selection. Once selected, the pillars supported the "big tent" of a stable catholic church and maintained within it different traditions that had come into existence after the death of Jesus.

The power that accrued to the bishop of Rome is a case in point. A city gained power and prestige if one of the original apostles evangelized there. Peter and Paul preached and were martyred in Rome, and subsequently her bishops traced their authority back to them. Because Rome was the capital of the empire and its wealthiest city, other cities and their congregations throughout Europe and Asia looked to Rome when disputes arose and when money was short. As the Roman congregation obliged them with doctrinal advice and funds for their ministries, the authority of Rome grew naturally on account of these advantages.

Even as Rome's authority increased, there was great instability of belief before a canon was established. Most sects had written forms of their traditions by AD 100. Christians of this period, Johnson writes, were more aware than later Church councils that some of the texts were fraudulent. Marcion made it his mission to separate the true from the false. Early leaders of the Church, however, realized that Marcion, though faithful to Paul, pruned too much, and he was forced to leave Rome. Without the Old Testament, a text with which Paul was thoroughly familiar, the context for a historical Jesus would have disappeared. In a reaction to Marcion the canon was opened up in late 2nd Century. Tertullian offers "a unique glimpse into the workings of the early church" because he checked a radical Hellenization of Jesus. Like Paul, he found the universality of Jesus in the spirit, not in a rational pruning of this or that text. Due to these circumstances and considerations, the New Testament canon included four gospels from different traditions. To those modern commentators who like to point out the many inconsistencies between the different narratives as a reason for discrediting them all, it helps to remember Tertullian's credo that he believes because it is absurd. Modern intellectuals are looking for something the Christian matrix was not intended to give.

Johnson notes that the expanded canon was a weapon against heresy. Once a tradition was brought into the big tent, orthodox leaders were able to gradually exclude those documents "penetrated by gnosticism" over a period of 300 years. This was one of several strategies. Another saved Paul for the New Testament. For a time Paul's authority was damaged by association with Marcion; by crediting him with "pastoral epistles" more in keeping with orthodoxy, his position in the canon was restored. The gospel of John was saved from an association with the heresy of Montanism by attributing to him three orthodox epistles. In addition, there was "horse trading" between East and West concerning Alexandrian and Roman documents. By 367, Johnson concludes, the process was complete. "By this time, the New Testament, roughly as we know it, had largely superseded the old Hebrew scriptures as the principal teaching instrument of the church. It was an instrument which had been fashioned by the Church, rather than vice versa."

B. The Christian Life

Paul's message had been quite simple: since the parousia was imminent, one must repent and have faith in the risen Jesus. When the parousia didn't come, however, Paul's crisis management gave way to the more "complicated and subtle" idea of the Christian life. Johnson has written an important passage (one of many in the book) to explain the significance of the shift:

> *"Thus the regulation of life once more tended to be portrayed as the condition of salvation and the great ethical commandment of the gospels assumed the status of new law. But law implied obedience; and obedience implied authority. What was this authority? The Church. What constituted the Church? The men who ran it."*

Similarly, the New Testament defined faith for an institutional church, and, more importantly, it determined the way these texts would be interpreted. Once a sacred canon had been selected, it had to be explained:

> *"...and the explanation itself was authoritative. Who was in charge of the process? The Church. What was the Church? The men who ran it."*

Johnson's short, crisp questions and answers explain the Church's rise as a mighty fortress.

In the early years of the Church bishops and deacons were charismatics with purely spiritual functions, but by AD 100 the primitive democracy of the early period was replaced with a "clerical structure." For the next 100 years the Church was "a haven for a wide spectrum of opinion," but it began to change around AD 200 as orthodoxy achieved a critical mass. The growing power and wealth of the Church exposed the need for a more "deliberate thinking out of policy," and this need was addressed by Origen of Alexandria and Cyprian of Carthage. Origen created an intellectual framework for the Christian life, and Cyprian showed how that framework could be implemented. As a philosopher Origen set down "the first theory of knowledge from within Christian assumptions," and he exalted ecclesiastical office along with an exalted Church as a sacred medium between God and man. With that framework in place thanks to the tireless efforts of Origen, Cyprian of Carthage devised a practical system of absolute control. Johnson's description of the "machinery" that made the system work is worth quoting at length:

> The Church was a divine institution; the Bride of Christ; Mother Church, the mediatrix of all salvation. It was one, undivided and catholic. Only in association with her could Catholics have life. Outside her holy fellowship there was nothing but error and darkness. The sacraments, episcopal ordination, the confession of faith, even the Bible itself, lost their meaning if used outside the true Church. The Church was also a human, visible community, found only in organized form. The individual could not be saved by direct contact with God. The carefully graded hierarchy, without which the organized Church could not exist, was established by Christ and the apostles. The laity was allowed to be present at the election of the bishop but the actual choice was made by all the presbyters...Without the office of bishop there could be no Church; and without the Church, no salvation...He interpreted the scriptures in the light of the Church's needs in any given situation...With Cyprian, then, the freedom preached by Paul and based on the power of Christian truth was removed from the ordinary members of the Church; it was retained only by the bishops, through whom the Holy Spirit still worked, who were collectively delegated to represent the totality of Church members.

While Johnson acknowledges this system as a form of absolute control, he ends the first chapter on a more positive note. He argues that there was no "element of planning" in these developments. "They suggest, rather, a series of ad hoc responses to actual situations," and they also reflect the intent of Christianity's founder to initiate a religion that would be "all things to all men." In the struggle with gnostic heresies and the free lancing of charismatics it survived "by avoiding extremes, by compromise, by developing an urbane temperament and erecting secular-type structures to preserve its unity and conduct its business."

Part Three: A Comic Vision

True Government Begins in Self-Government

Johnson's observation that the Church managed its mission with "secular-type structures" suggests that his history is an inquiry into Western forms of government as well as a study of Christianity. A review of themes discussed in the previous essays adds more evidence for this interpretation.

A Comic Vision of Great Constancy and the essays in this volume argue that a moral order exists and that true government begins in self-government in accordance with that order. This insight and the secular structures to which Johnson refers both have deep roots in Christianity. According to Johnson, Jesus understood that, to become a universal religion, Judaism had to be reformed. He preached to the Am Ha-Aretz, the people of the land, "a new message of salvation through love, sacrifice and faith." He would move them with his words and charisma to change their outlook about life and to be their best selves. People went to him for inspiration and healing. Adam Smith was also concerned with what moves us to do what we do; it's why he wrote *The Theory of Moral Sentiments*. He points out that, because we want to be loved and to be lovely (to deserve the love we receive), we learn to regulate our own behaviors.

Those who depreciate the power of our moral sentiments may think a social order depends almost entirely on a formal system of legislation, laws, law courts, and law enforcement. Paul enforced the law like this before he encountered the risen Christ on the road to Damascus. After the encounter, though, he traveled from one end of the empire to the other exhorting gentiles to be guided by the Holy Spirit as he himself had been ever since his vision. If we put Paul and Adam Smith side by side, Smith's theory of moral sentiments appears to have been written in a similar, but more secular, spirit. Whether it's by virtue of the spirit or by the impartial spectator, people are moved to govern themselves.

Like *The Theory of Moral Sentiments*, *The Great Debate* by Yuval Levin is an inquiry into what makes people tick, as Roberts puts it. It's an issue that a political philosophy must address, for we are governed by what matters most to us in our lives. By putting Edmund Burke's ideas side by side with Paul's vision, it's clear that Burke's ideas have much in common with the donation of life and the obligation of love that were the constant subjects of Paul's letters. Caring for a baby or an elderly parent is what a rational person does. It doesn't reflect the wisdom or the choice of an individual. It reflects the wisdom of the predisposed order of things. Translated into the language of sentiments, it points to love as a prime mover. Just as Adam Smith's theory may have its roots in a Judeo-Christian vision of self-government (which finds a sweet spot between the law and the spirit), Edmund Burke's description of citizens fulfilling their essential obligations and relations, especially family relations, may have its roots in Paul's vision of a community constituted by the donation of life and the obligations of love. I say "may have" because these sentences are developing the implications of an analogy rather than a causal relation. My inquiry into these matters is more art than science, as should be clear by now.

Direct Contact

A. Encountering the Word Made Flesh

This essay begins with Johnson's judgment that the teaching of Jesus is "more a series of glimpses, or matrices, a collection of insights, rather than a code of doctrine." Despite this difficulty, Johnson wonders at how "the personality behind the mission is in no way fragmented but is always integrated and true to character." Johnson wrote his history, I believe, to show that the subsequent history of Christianity reflects the integrity of these matrices and insights. Out of many glimpses we are given a sense of the man and the church he founded.

Paul's letters are about a life transformed by an encounter with the risen Christ. For Paul, direct contact with Christianity's founder was essential. For this reason, church leaders who came after him understood that a gnostic movement like the Docetists posed a great danger to the character of Jesus and to his church. Docetists denied that He had "ever been man: his body was semblance or dokesis." To gain popularity with cosmopolitan gentiles who "found it hard to understand why Christianity should wish or need to maintain the Jewish connection," they Hellenized the movement by cutting Jesus off from his historical roots and turning him into an idea. The early church strongly opposed their interpretation. As a man Jesus had a history with a place in history; as God he represented the fulfillment of history. Just as a sense of history and God's hand in it are essential to Judaism, the early church decided that Jesus had to be understood within his historical context, and so they made the Old Testament the first half of the Christian Bible.

But how do Christians after Paul make direct contact? Johnson's history suggests that the answer isn't simple, just as Jesus himself isn't simple. An institutional church—its sacraments, buildings, calendar, rituals, and consecrated bishops—rescued the Jesus movement at a time when it might easily have dissolved into disparate cults. These attributes contributed then and for hundreds of years after the initial rescue to the sense that, once inside this mighty fortress, a believer was in relationship with a physical presence. The Word of God in the Christian Bible offered as well a presence within that most intimate theater, the consciousness of an individual, especially when His word was translated into the vernacular and published in Bibles the laity could study. The word of God proved to be decisive for many in the time of the Reformation. For them, the insubstantial pageant of the institutional church faded as if it had been a dream (a bad one), and the conscience of Everyman became his Church.

Can anyone say definitively which path, an institutional church or the word of God, leads to a more direct contact? When he comes to that part of his history, Johnson doesn't take sides. From his telling of the story the two sides together still abide within the founder's matrix despite efforts to separate them. Johnson wrote a chapter called "The Third Force" to feature Erasmus as the author and the hero of that vision. Just as Jesus simplified Judaism to make it more universal, Erasmus worked to bring the church closer to its founder, who lived and taught among the people of the land. He regarded it "as normal and desirable that educated laymen should play their full part in the direction of the church and declined absolutely to endorse an exclusive role for the clergy." To downplay divisive differences in doctrine, Erasmus favored a faith with a minimum of theology and "stressed man's capacity to use his own resources to work out his salvation." He was a popularizer as well as a serious scholar. At the end of the book, Johnson even speculates, in the spirit of Erasmus, that the divisions within the church could someday be mended.

B. Death and Rebirth in Comedy

As I define it in my readings of Chaucer and Shakespeare, a comic vision has much in common with Paul's vision of the risen Christ; to get the most out of life we must die to live. Paul witnessed that for Jesus this was literally the case, and it's believed that Paul himself was martyred in Rome. Comedy, however, puts the notion of dying to live within the context of everyday life. Because the ideas to which we are attached— about politics, individual rights, our self image, ownership of a property, "ownership" of a lover, or "ownership" of a child—swell to gigantic proportions, human beings experience the loss of an attachment as a kind of death. Since everyone has had these experiences and lived through them, we learn as well that it's a kind of death which can lead to renewed life. From personal experience I have argued that a comic fall is the greatest teacher because it speaks to us directly, physically. We learn its lessons, not just through rote memorization or recollections in tranquility, but in the flesh.

While teaching English in a public school, I discovered two great things about the wisdom of comedy. Because it's non-sectarian, it brings people together. I also learned, through painful trials and errors of my own and through the success comedy had in the classroom, to appreciate a form which helps us to hear the voice of wisdom when it calls to us in the affairs of everyday life. Usually, it calls to tell us that we're in the middle of making a serious mistake. People of any age need that voice confirmed and fleshed out through a vehicle for understanding—whether it's a person, a church, the rule of law, or a text. The confirmations are a critical part of self-government.

In his climactic speech at the end of "The Knight's Tale" Chaucer's Theseus explains to his people why he is able to speak to them about "the First Great Cause and Mover of All above":

> I need not quote authority or raise
> More proof than what experience can show,
> But give opinion from what I know.

He knows what he knows from the trials and errors of experience. Our slip ups and mistakes are physically uncomfortable, whether it's our bottom or our pride that's injured. When we slip up and fall from casual or willful inattention, the ground of our existence rushes up to meet our bodies, and the rush of awareness that comes of this meeting smacks of wisdom. But over time we lose its meaning unless it's confirmed in some way. It requires a larger context, a repository of trials and errors that speaks to us cogently of Everyman's falls. We need a human voice, a wise counselor like Theseus, to speak of it.

C. The History of Christianity as Comedy

After Paul of Tarsus, Erasmus is the second most important hero in Johnson's history of his faith. Fifteen hundred years after its founding, five hundred years ago and at a time when the medieval church was breaking up, Erasmus wrote *The Praise of Folly* to save Christianity with a comic vision. Unlike most encomiums where a person is praised by someone else, Erasmus has Folly stand up in a crowd in order to praise herself with a brazenness that typifies the folly of Folly. She must be a popular speaker, for the crowd recognizes and greets her with smiles and cheers.

Like Chaucer's Wife of Bath, Folly praises herself with gusto and great wit, but her character changes as she surveys folly in all the walks of life. By the end, she has become the voice of wisdom, for "Has not God made foolish the wisdom of the world" (1 Corinthians 1:20). Paul's sentence can be read both ways. The so-called wisdom of the world, the domain of intellectuals, is mere foolishness; these philosophers love their own ideas more than life itself. Conversely, the faith that human life can be a comedy requires the simplicity of a merry heart, the foolishness of God, which "doeth good like a medicine" (Proverbs 17:22). The foolish Wife of Bath may seem to be separated from the apostle Paul by an unbridgeable gap, but both Chaucer and Erasmus saw the connection. (The Wife even refers to Paul in the Prologue of her tale.) Shakespeare saw it, too. His most famous example of it, *A Midsummer Night's Dream,* depends on the divine fool Bottom for its comic ending. Since folly makes itself felt everywhere in the world, it's a virtue with a physical value.

As Erasmus did before him, Johnson still finds that Christianity embodies the only kind of freedom that matters and conveys timeless reassurance that human beings are capable of arranging their affairs in time for a comic conclusion. Johnson wrote *Modern Times* to document the industrial scale bloodshed and the manifest failures of government in the twentieth Century, and yet he gave his narrative a comic structure, as I've explained in my essay on it. We should not forget that millions of ordinary people, like Bottom, cracked open the Iron Curtain in massive popular demonstrations. Reading and writing about his history of Christianity in the year AD 2016, when there's a strong sense that something important is breaking up all around us, I imagine that Johnson wrote his book for a time like this and that he would have us read it as a comedy.

As a comedy is for its characters, Johnson's history is a forthright presentation of Christianity's trials and errors. The lessons learned over the many centuries serve to instruct us in our own time, for they have to do with timeless group dynamics. I've singled out two of them for special emphasis. We learn from the history of the church to avoid the gnostic error of inflexibly ordering our life by superhuman standards. We are flesh and blood human beings with strong human sentiments, not an image or idea. No one idea (or a basketful of them) can denote us truly. The reductive gnostic tendency is alive and well in modern life, but now as then an obsessive attachment to an image or idea can't cure the body or the body politic except as an accelerant for the eventual flame out.

We also learn to beware of free lancing charismatics. Johnson observes that "The nature of Christianity, carried rapidly forward by wandering evangelists, attracted charlatans." Lucian, an early critic of Christians said of them that "they take their beliefs from tradition, and do not insist on definite evidence. Any professional fraud can impose on them and make a lot of money very quickly." The institutional church evolved to counteract the tendency charismatics have of flying off centrifugally in their own direction.

Fast forwarding over a thousand years, we read that some took Luther's reforms to mean that Everyman was his own priest, and, since he was his own priest, it surely must follow that Everyman was his own king as well. A 16th Century populist leader like Thomas Muntzer was a fanatic, not a fraudster. He preached in Saxony that the royal priesthood of the common man would smash the established order of Pope and King, and he invited the princes of Germany to "join the covenanted people in overthrowing the Antichrist." A charismatic like Muntzer believed, as early Christians did, that the parousia "would mark the beginning of eternal and perfect government," and so he advocated a violent apocalypse to hasten the end. For Johnson, Muntzer's preaching prefigures the ideology of class warfare and bloody convulsion which proved so destructive in the 20th Century. This time, though, totalitarian movements charged with an evangelical fervor attached themselves to reductive, pseudo-scientific social theories and became political vehicles that would appeal to both charismatics and gnostics. The marriage of these elements may explain why the movements have been so successful and so deadly.

Extremes are the villains in Johnson's narrative but as always the villains play a useful role in the story. They illustrate that Christianity survived "by avoiding extremes, by compromise, by developing an urbane temperament and erecting secular-type structures to preserve its unity and conduct its business." Since I've been studying and writing about his history during the course of the 2016 Presidential campaigns, I find that Johnson's depiction of these extremes, the rigid ideologues and the free lancing charismatics, outlines fault lines present in our own politics.

D. A Comic Vision of Time

How does an ordinary person make direct contact with the Holy Spirit? Christians have wrestled for two millennia with the question. In a similar spirit comedy is concerned with how we make direct contact with a friend, a loved one, or an enemy; with the objects and obligations of everyday life; with the spirit of Chaucer and Shakespeare; with the faithfulness of dogs and other miracles of nature. As Christianity does, comedy teaches that the question will involve a change in the way we love, our desire for the things of this world. An intense desire for direct contact underlies the question about how it's made.

Like a telescope, microscope, or prescription glasses, the poetry of Chaucer and Shakespeare helps us to observe the operations of desire. We learn from their poetic instruments, for example, that time and desire are one substance. At the bottom of their inquiry is a simple proposition: Human beings desire what they don't have; an obstacle separates the two. Because human beings are creators and image makers, we can imagine having the object. The not-having is now one moment, and the having is another. The two images together suggest a trip which involves going from point A to point B, and this trip will take time. From the perspective of point A, time is the obstacle; time is the frustration, a form of hate, we feel in the face of desire.

In the opening lines of *A Midsummer Night's Dream* Theseus gives voice to this frustration:

Now fair Hippolyte, our nuptial hour
Draws on apace; four happy days bring in
Another moon. But oh, methinks how slow
This old moon wanes! She lingers my desires,
Like to a stepdame, or a dowager,
Long withering out a young man's revenue.

Theseus is a soldier. He's used to fighting and killing obstacles to his will. Here, though, he fights an invisible and unconquerable enemy, the four days that separate him from the consummation of their marriage. (The fact that he chooses to characterize Time as a woman is grist for the mill in my reading of the play.) Since desire will always involve what we don't have and since we hate the obstacle to our love, love and hate are as inextricably linked in the operations of desire as desire and time.

Hippolyta replies with a vision of timeless power and beauty:

Four days will quickly steep themselves in night
Four nights will quickly dream away the time,
And then the moon, like to a silver bow
New bent in heaven, shall behold the night
of our solemnities.

Through the might of her vision, where she can imagine the progress of their solemnities from the moon's point of view, time simply vanishes, and all the problems of her impatient lover dissolve along with everything else. There's nothing left to be an obstacle (that is, until Theseus considers what that moon, like the silver bow of the huntress Diana, might mean for him when he becomes aware that it's the only thing left in his life). The consummation Theseus or anyone seeks involves a death (the death of time) and a rebirth into (for lack of a better word) timelessness.

Theseus speaks as a lover and vents the frustrations lovers feel in intimate relations. Because he's the ruler of Athens, however, he wears two caps, that of a lover and that of a duke. Within moments of uttering the lines above, he's thrust into a dispute between a father and a daughter which, as chief magistrate of the land, he must adjudicate. It's a difficult case which involves the happiness, even the life, of the girl, and it throws an obstacle up between himself and the civil peace he desires as the appropriate setting for his marriage. Just as Theseus resents the time that separates him from the consummation of his love, it's clear he resents the dispute of the father and daughter and the time he must devote to it.

These observations about the nature of love don't argue for passivity or pacifism. Quite the contrary. We are all lovers and fighters whether we like it or not. In the affairs of everyday life good men fight tyrants. At the beginning of "The Knight's Tale," Chaucer's Theseus drops everything, even his wedding night, and rides through the night to oppose the tyrant Creon. Shakespeare's Theseus and Chaucer's Theseus are both worthy men, and good men take it upon themselves to judge a case as best they can and fight tyrants to the death. The fighting and the judging, though, require a kind of double vision. Practical soldiers and judges need an eye for that which can be gained over time and an eye for that which is timeless and already present.

From a study of Christianity, we learn that this double vision touches on an important issue in the early years of the church. For some, the coming of God as man to earth meant that the kingdom had come, that time (in which there was death from Adam) and creation had been redeemed. For others it meant that a process of salvation had been initiated. They waited on the Second Coming which would be its consummation. In Romans 8: 24-25 Paul observes the difference between being in and out of time: "Who hopes for what they already have? But if we hope for what we do not have, we wait for it patiently." Even though he still lives in time, the spirit, which is timeless, abides in him, and so he can be patient. As Paul did, we glimpse here the elusive form of wisdom and of a comic conclusion.

Time in the modern world has become a monolith of gigantic

proportions, and we worship it in public places like Times Square on special occasions like New Year's Eve. But in worshipping it as the overlord of life, we build the obstacle that most separates us from what we desire. That is until, like a bolt out of the blue, something touches us directly and dissolves the baseless fabric of time's dominion. The comic vision of scripture, Chaucer, and Shakespeare reminds us that wisdom is timeless, no less present than it was at the beginning.

With such an emphasis on time by the cultural establishment, alternative cultures, that delight in their difference, have made timelessness an object of cult worship; in new age venues all over the world we're told by teachers in-the-know to be in-the-moment. It's something easy enough to say, but the student who would carry out the command runs headlong into the double bind of consciousness undoing consciousness, which is as easy as picking oneself up by one's own bootstraps. Instead, we learn from better counselors that self-government means patience, and patience develops as a way to survive and prosper in the passionate arena of love and hate.

EPILOGUE

I've put Claude Lorrain's "The Return of Odysseus" on the cover of this book mainly because it's a beautiful painting. I hoped it would arrest a reader's attention as it did mine. The story it tells and its relationship to the story Homer tells are also of interest. Due to the gods' intervention, Homer's Odysseus comes to Ithaca sound asleep in the stern of the Phaeacians' ship. They drop him off still asleep on a remote part of the island, and when he wakes Athena disguises him as a beggarly Nobody that nobody will notice when he goes to town. His individuality as Odysseus is asleep, and instead he's full of the gods who have brought him back and readied him to regain his kingdom. Where is Odysseus in Lorrain's picture? I've looked, and I can't find him. He may be on board the ship coming into the harbor, but that's only suggested. By frustrating our intent, the painter invites us to imagine the return of Odysseus as Nobody. The rightful king, he has brought with him the wisdom gained from twenty years of war and wandering, but he's there as an invisible presence. Already a great peace has settled over the island as the people go about their business.

Like the return of Odysseus the opening lines of Proverbs 8 assures us that a moral order exists:

> Does not wisdom call out?
>> Does not understanding raise her voice?
> At the highest point along the way,
>> where the paths meet, she takes her stand;
> beside the gate leading into the city,
>> at the entrance, she cries aloud:
> "To you, O people, I call out;
>> I raise my voice to all mankind."

The opening line of Proverbs 8 serves as the title of Chapter Ten, and Blake's print "Ancient of Days" which illustrates it refers to verse 27. In the King James version Wisdom explains:

> *The Lord possessed me in the beginning of his way,*
>   *before his works of old.*
> *I was set up from everlasting,*
>   *from the beginning*
>   *or ever the earth was.*
> *When there were no depths, I was brought forth;*
>   *when there were no fountains abounding with water.*
> *Before the mountains were settled,*
>   *before the hills was I brought forth:*
> *while as yet he had not made the earth, nor the fields,*
>   *nor the highest part of the dust of the world.*
> *When he prepared the heavens, I was there:*
>   *when he set a compass upon the face of the depth:*
> *When he established the clouds above:*
>   *when he strengthened the fountains of the deep...*

Blake's striking image expresses the matrix of spirit and reason that animates Johnson's history of Christianity. The Lord is the spiritual primal source of all. Wisdom assures us, though, that she is present as well even if we don't see her in the picture. She's present especially, I imagine, in the compass, the instrument for measurement and for knowing. Because we live in time, harried and rushed by the pressure of it, and tend not to hear the voice that calls to us in the marketplace where the paths and people meet, the image reminds us that the compass is an extension of the "strong hand and outstretched arm" that liberated human beings from slavery. We need to be reminded. Wisdom, therefore, calls to us in our language, which is as much a miracle as creation itself and set up from everlasting, to set us right.

PHOTO CREDITS

Cover: Claude Lorrain's *The Return of Odysseus,*
Art Resource

Chapter One: Warwick Goble's *Sita Finds Rama Among the Lotus Blooms,*
Art Resource

Chapter Two: Nicholas Poussin's *Echo and Narcissus,*
Art Resource

Chapter Three: Hendrick Martensz Sorgh's *The Vegetable Market,*
The Rijksmuseum Museum

Chapter Four: Thomas Cole's *Interior of the Colosseum, Rome,*
Albany Institute of History

Chapter Five: *Ulysses and the Sirens* Roman mosaic from Dougga,
Art Resource

Chapter Six: Pieter Bruegel's *The Harvesters,*
Art Resource

Chapter Seven: Michelangelo's panel of *The Great Flood* from the Sistine
Chapel, Art Resource

Chapter Eight: M.C. Escher's *Relativity,* © 2016 The M.C. Escher Company-
The Netherlands. All rights reserved.
www.mcescher.com

Chapter Nine: Fra Angelica's *The Conversion of St. Augustine,*
Art Resource

Chapter Ten and Back Cover: William Blake's *Ancient of Days,*
Art Resource

| A Comic Vision of Self-Government